I0160519

TIMELESSNESS

Conversations on Life, Literature, Spirituality, and Culture

James G. Cowan and
Arthur Versluis

Shining through these conversations between two remarkable writers and thinkers is a deeply felt need for a re-enchantment of the world, a rediscovery of the sacred in the landscape and a reconnection with our spiritual roots. The re-enchantment of the world may still be possible!
—Christopher McIntosh, author of *The Rosicrucians*, *Gardens of the Gods*, and *Beyond the North Wind.*

The offspring of two scintillating minds and their lifelong friendship, these timely and timeless conversations cover many engaging topics, ranging from ancient sacred sites and landscapes, traditional ways of knowing, to the spiritual rebirth of literature and culture, and even what it means to be a real writer of substance in today's world. Very highly recommended.
— David Fideler, author of *Restoring the Soul of the World*

Such conversations as these are a rarity—cultured, eloquent, and deeply rewarding. Two friends—two lifelong explorers of sacred landscapes—in stimulating discussion. A worthy final testament to the life and thought of author and troubadour James Cowan.
—Kingsley L. Dennis, author of *The Sacred Revival* and many other books.

Library of Congress Cataloging-in-Publication Data
Names: Cowan, James, 1942- author. | Versluis, Arthur, 1959- author.
Title: Timelessness : conversations on life, literature, spirituality, and culture / James G Cowan and Arthur Versluis.
Description: Minneapolis, MN : New Cultures Press, 2020. | Series: Hieros ; 1 Identifiers: LCCN 2020000479 (print) | LCCN 2020000480 (ebook) | ISBN 9781596500310 (hardcover) | ISBN 9781596500334 (paperback) | ISBN 9781596500327 (epub)
Subjects: LCSH: Light--Religious aspects. | Time--Religious aspects. | Spirituality--Aboriginal Australians. | Aboriginal Australians--Civilization. | Cowan, James, 1942---Interviews.
Classification: LCC BL265.L5 C69 2020 (print) | LCC BL265.L5 (ebook) |
DDC 824/.914--dc23
LC record available at https://lccn.loc.gov/2020000479
LC ebook record available at https://lccn.loc.gov/2020000480

27 26 25 24 23 22 21 20   10 9 8 7 6 5 4 3 2 1

New Cultures Press
Minneapolis, MN
www.newcultures.org
www.hieros.world

Contents

Introduction

Arthur Versluis

James Cowan and I were friends for decades. We were introduced to one another by the British poet and literary critic Kathleen Raine, who told me that there was a remarkable Australian writer whom I should certainly meet. He and I began a correspondence that became the bond of an enduring friendship. We met at various places around the world, he came to visit me in the United States, I came to visit him and his wife in Australia, and throughout all the vicissitudes, joys, and triumphs of life, we shared one another's lives, confided in one another, encouraged each other to grow, did all that friends could do for one another. He lived fully, wholeheartedly. He said that his element was fire.

When first we met, Jim was an experienced adventurer. He had explored the wilds of Borneo and been among headhunters; he had gone far into the Australian desert outback, and been among the Aborigines; he had gone to New York and London; he had worked on a dodgy Middle Eastern air flight company; he had had all manner of adventures. His adventurous nature came naturally to him, from his ancestors who came to Australia from Ireland, and from his father in particular, who was a flight navigator for Qantas. Jim was an inveterate traveler, a rolling stone who could not stay in one place too long. In those early years of our friendship, Jim rode endurance rides in the Australian outback on his flighty Arabian horse, through the most wild of country.

He was already a novelist, but in addition to writing fiction, he began to explore Aboriginal ways of understanding the remote and harsh Australian landscape, in books like *Sacred Places in Australia*, *Mysteries of the Dream-time: The Spiritual Life of Australian Aborigines*, and *Aborigine Dreaming: An Introduction to the Wisdom and Magic of the Aboriginal Traditions*. I have on my wall a gift from him, the first Aboriginal painting of the Dreaming that he had gotten, done on bark by an Aboriginal elder in the 1970s, long before the idea of Aboriginal painting of sacred landscapes became more widely known.

I remember being awakened in the middle of the night—I think it was around three in the morning—by a telephone call from Jim in which, bewildered and still groggy, I heard his excited voice explaining that he and his wife Wendy were going to go off to Balgo, Australia, in the outback, in order to live among the Aborigines. And indeed, they did exactly that, living in an Aboriginal community at Balgo, making it possible for the Aborigines to paint acrylic versions of their traditional Dreaming places. These paintings pioneered that genre of Aboriginal art. And Jim and Wendy came away with many entertaining stories of this period, the first of their sojourns in unusual places.

In the mid-1990s, Jim published *Mapmaker's Dream: The Meditations of Fra Mauro*, and then two years later, *A Troubadour's Testament*. These were the breakthrough books in which Jim began to explore his signature style that combined historical research, limpid prose, and a distinctive use of narrator's voice with a slight surrealism. *Mapmaker's Dream* won the Australian Gold Medal for Literature, and those two books brought him and his work into the public eye in a different way, with much critical praise.

Later, they moved to a small town in Italy, where Jim researched and wrote various books, including *Francis: A Saint's Way*, and began to explore his mature understanding of what literature could be. During this period, he continued to write fiction, and it was during this time that he began to develop what he later came to term "metaphysical realism." After returning to Australia, they then moved to Argentina, spending time in the country of Jorge Luis Borges, immersing themselves in its distinctive combination of European and Latin American cultures.

Eventually, they moved back to Australia, near the idyllic community of Byron Bay, where Jim was to refine his masterwork, the Kingdoms trilogy, a series of three interlinked novels that together brought into being the mature form of his distinctive literary perspective, deeply imbued with his vast erudition and cultural knowledge garnered from a lifetime of sojourns and adventures around the world. In these books, he expressed his vision of what literature could be, not just as a reflection of the physical world, but rather as a flowering of the full range of human life, including its spiritual dimensions.

During their time near Byron Bay, Jim continued to write, non-fiction as well as fiction and poetry, including an array of essays on disparate topics including mysticism, technology, what he had learned from Aborigines over the decades, and much else. It was the period in which he began to sum up and complete his life's work as a writer. He completed a Ph.D. from the University of Queensland, his thesis later published as a scholarly monograph, *Hamlet's Ghost*. And during this period he encouraged the development of a local intellectual community via occasional Philosophy Café events that brought in dozens, sometimes up to a hundred people for lively, open discussion.

It was then that he was diagnosed with cancer, and although he underwent various kinds of treatment, it inexorably began to take its toll on him. But he remained intellectually alive and engaged with the community in Byron Bay, as well as with a wide range of correspondents and contacts around the world. And he continued to write other works, including poems and essays. He was always reading and writing, an explorer of the mind, too.

In this latter phase I flew to be with him and Wendy, and brought along a digital audio recorder. We had had so many extraordinary conversations over the years, but this now had a special quality because we knew that the end of his physical life was not too far away. Though I was there longer, on five days, each day in the morning, outside in the courtyard, with the exotic birds in the background, we spoke about the themes that brought together his life's work, about how his Aboriginal contacts and his highly cultured literary and philosophical life intersected with his fiction, and about what advice he had for a young writer.

We were well aware, of course, that the dialogue is

itself a classical form, and that in our conversations, we were participating in a form that went back to Plato, and that recurred throughout Western philosophical and literary history. Giordano Bruno wrote dialogues; so did Schelling; so did many others. It is very much an exchange—that is, I am participating in the conversation just as he is—and through our back and forth, something very distinctive emerges. It is, in part, a summary of his life's work.

People commonly take "genius" nowadays to refer to what one "is," as a prodigy, often someone with a particular kind of knack, for instance, an uncanny ability to make money or to invent gizmos. And of course, those things are achievements of a sort. But the word "genius" originally referred to someone's inner spirit, the distinctive life force and animating power that makes that individual unique and full of life. Plotinus's genius was said to be a god. Here, I will say that in the ancient sense, Jim was full of genius. You can hear it clearly in the audio, for that matter. Hence the title: for the conversations are about the intersection of timelessness and time.

Jim also was fully cultured in the most profound sense. I realize that a term like this is out of fashion, but in truth, it is never truly out of vogue because it expresses a refined and erudite sensibility, one that incorporates all the life experience and knowledge from disparate sources one has attained over the years into one's full being. It expresses not only an intellectual, but also a realized spiritual aspect of one's nature.

A close friend who heard these conversations in audio form wrote me and said that they were a moving experience, particularly the last one, the advice to a young writer. Why? In part, no doubt, because in it, Jim is conveying his life's experience as a writer to someone who seeks to be a writer, to take up where he is leaving off. It is in some sense, his testament, his bequest to us. And it is also empowering, meaning that he is handing the baton to you, dear reader, should you wish to take it up.

In what follows, you get a sense of this most refined and remarkable of men, and through what is here, you can participate in our conversations too. It is not limited to its thematic topics but, as a set of conversations, has much deeper and wider ramifications than might first appear. Let it be, come back to it, let it all percolate. These truly are conversations about life, about how to live, and what to live for, about literature, spirituality, and culture. I hope you treasure them as much as we do. Enjoy!

First Conversation:

OUROBOROS

JC: I've been thinking about our discussion yesterday with regard to megalithic culture. I thought to myself what parallel courses you and I are taking. You went back to megalithic culture in Europe, starting the process of uncovering the strange and remarkable part of our shared European deep culture, and that struck me as very important because I had done the same by going back in Aboriginal culture and it was the same impetus—the feeling that in a sense, if you didn't come to grips with the culture that understood its landscape, then you were not ever going to understand the landscape that you inhabited in a deeper way. And so in many cases, those books of mine were always about this sense of going back into the ancient pre-text environment to see what could be derived with regard to caves, rock-art, petroglyphs—all these standing stones in the far West, which I encountered up in the Kimberly, and I do remember how this experience affected me. It was not just an abstract engagement with the search. You did that at one level, but I always think as a creative writer, you've got to hold to that as one of the pillars by which you operate, yet you also need to move into that area of intuition and empathy, which then determine how you integrate the rational into the surreal, which is the other world.

And so when I was doing the work out in the bush, I experienced powerful sensations in these places. Sometimes, in fact, I had to move the tent because it was too powerful to camp on and I remember being out at Winbaraku, which is where I'd like my ashes to be thrown, and I remember we would camp by this great snake Jarapiri. Colin Beard [Jim's photographer friend] was in his tent and I was in my tent, because by that stage, we were living in separate tents [laughs] since he snored, I didn't, or the other way around, I can't remember now. But anyway, when I was camped there, I heard the voices from that stone serpent, which was really a giant megalith with a snake on it. There are many stories with regard to the dingo as well as the snake. I woke up in the morning and said to Colin, I can't sleep near it any more. We're going to have to move our tents further away. The Aborigines had dropped us out there, you see. They had spent the day there with us and told us the stories and I said to the Aboriginal custodian, do you mind if we camp here? He said no, but you'll have to take me back to town. I said that's good, so there were three or four old men whom I negotiated with at a community about thirty kilometers away and they agreed to take us out there in order to photograph it and to get the stories, but when you encounter that kind of rock formation, it does radiate the numen. There's no doubt about it. It's numen and I felt this very powerfully, particularly when—see, this is the thing I'm trying to get to—when you're with the custodians, there is a voice for those stones, which is not what you're experiencing in the wider theater of European megaliths because there's nobody around there.

AV: There isn't a living interpreter or messenger or carrier of the tradition other than you. You, by your presence alone, *are* that. That's actually comparable to the Native American sites that I've been to, where again, even though I've been to many Native American sites, sometimes with someone who is an elder in the tradition, not often, but in those cases as well, they're not custodians in the way you're talking about. There's little continuity in the places that I've experienced. There is possibly continuity in some of the Native American ones. In Europe that's another matter, because there, you're talking about visiting megalithic formations or constructions that are 5,000, 7,000 years old—sometimes more than that—sometimes less, so it's incumbent on you by being there to open enough to be able to understand what's there and what's conveyed there directly. That's the challenge.

JC: It is a challenge and that's why I think we're into an area of discussion with regard to the transition from a pre-literate culture that's retained its essence within the stone so to speak, into a modern context because this is what we're really talking about. We're not just seeing them as historical or merely as artifacts. I don't anyway, you've seen that too. See the landscape as a vital expression of a mythic environment in which those custodians lived and live and it's that challenge facing you to find the language and that's going to be—that's the hardest thing you see—is to find the language to make that transition into a new form of literature. It's no good just saying well, we're going to write about megaliths and they've got a certain historical significance; you've got to get actually into it creatively—that's the big challenge of a writer I think with regard to this material. Does that make sense?

AV: It does and there's a difference between the kinds of sites that we're talking about. I remember my father and I went to an area of petroglyphs. The site has the most numerous petroglyphs in a single area in New Mexico and it was about three hours driving from where my parents' ranch is, so we drove there. This was just a few years ago, and we walked up—it was above White Sands, where they tested nuclear weapons—so in the distance there's an ocean of white and it's a ridge that runs in front of some mountains, so there's a line of mountains behind us, and then a ridge and you hike up. It's a national park now. And you walk up to the top and you walk along that trail at the very top and the petroglyphs are all around you or in front of you or beside you or sometimes below you on rocks. As you walk through, you begin to realize that it's encoded mystery—it's like an encoded Mystery tradition because around you are these images and you're walking through those images. And it's not my tradition in the sense that the people who are most connected to those petroglyphs are gone and there aren't local people who act as interpreters. It's very analogous to what we're talking about in Europe and as I walked through it with my father, I don't know what he saw really. He didn't comment on it, but what I saw were these petroglyphs not as images in a sort of modern sense of modern painting, but as initiatory, as the manifestations of an initiatory set of experiences as you walk through, because you're actually moving through these images. You're moving through living images and those images are of a sun, or of serpents, or birds, thunderbirds, and so on. And by walking through, you're participating in the reality that is conveyed by a petroglyph there connected to that direct experience hundreds, perhaps even in some cases thousands of years ago. You're participating in that experience by being there to some extent. Speaking for myself, I have a more direct connection to Western France or Cornwall or Ireland than I do to some of these Native American sites, but still, the experience is there. The numinosity is not as strong as in Europe. In Europe, I've had experiences that are very strong. So the difference I think between what we're talking about is partly also the degree of numinosity, you can say and maybe you can talk a little bit more about that—that experience of numinosity because I fully understand what you mean by moving the tent in order to not be—

JC: Tampering with the field.

AV:—yes, so immersed in that field as to sleep in it, because that's of course incubation. That's the practice of incubation, which is to sleep right next to a numinous place.

JC: Yes, of course you're right.

AV: And have dreams.

JC: And of course, in the nature of this experience, you're dealing with an ancient civilization, which is the Aboriginals. And when you rub up against their myth life, you recognize the difference between you and they, not only because of time, but in terms of space and in terms of culture. So when you suggest quite rightly that there's numinosity in places that's high, low, or medium, my sense is that it depends entirely upon the continued participation of a custodian or a group of people who look after the sites. So the sites have been nurtured like a gardener nurtures a garden. And Aboriginals are quite specific about that. They would argue that they are singing the souls of the place. When we sing them, we enliven the rock—the mountain. If we don't sing them, of course it becomes mute and the great fear among Aborigines is that the custodians of the songs have died or haven't passed on because of present-day circumstance, and so these places fall into a state of absolute muteness and no longer have any reality for anyone.

AV: In the living human world.

JC: In the living human world and so in a way, for writers and creators like ourselves, to go back into that world with the openness of an innocent, is very important because you can live in a rational world and approach it as I have with other people—make particular remarks—but I think if you allow yourself to actually enter as an initiate so to speak, these languages, these places, will speak to you. Very much so.

AV: They will. But some of these places that I'm referring to have been damaged and in one case, there is a megalithic site called in recent times the Hurlers. In the Second World War, US and British forces used tanks for practice, and they just rolled right over some of the Hurlers. And then they were reset. At the same time, there is a certain mysterious quality to that place, which is preserved, and it doesn't really—it doesn't depend on whether somebody ran over one of the megaliths or more with a tank any more than the sacrosanct nature of Samothrace, the great Mystery center, is affected by the fact that earthquakes and monotheists destroyed it stone by stone because the electric kind of numinosity that's there transcends the physical—it is so embedded in the very stones that it transcends the physical. And that's true of many of these places in my experience. So it's more a matter of being open.

JC: Well, that's what I was talking about. You need to have this—you walk into the open so to speak and I suspect that's how someone like Victor Segalen went to China and was completely affected by the Chinese experience: they were open too, and it's that sense of being open that I think has been lacking in literature for a long time. My sense is that we've forgotten what it is to be open in the literary sense too and that's where people like Segalen, myself, and others come into play because we do live in the open, as you pointed out earlier. But my sense too—I always wanted—it was one of my dreams was to take you to this place—and it still is entirely possible in a crazy sort of way, because I wanted us to visit those sacred sites, which are in their own way, megaliths—

AV: In the Flinders Range.

JC: Yes, and *Sacred Places in Australia* is a very remarkable book because it shows you all of the places—and the informants—the women and men that inform—the maps and the photographs of the megalithic environments that these are in. What a wonderful journey for us to do, and I still dream of that because I still want to go back to the Flinders and my brother of course has all the gear and that—it would be a wonderful thing to do. Look at that back cover image and the sense of megalithic landscape it conveys. I always dreamt of our taking those journeys and so I brought that set of images for you to look at—even to tantalize and take away with you, and also to give you an insight into the great literary tradition here in a story through that book. Those are just the slides you can look at. But my sense is that there is a language there of these petroglyphs, these megaliths, these stone encasements of spirits that has yet to be given its language for the twenty-first century, and that's what I'm talking about. And that's where the creative process—it's like—and this is talking in a purely literary fashion, is that you're trying to take your mind and re-jerk it into a new way of actually thinking and that's the hardest thing, when you're breaking into a new language or trying to get into a new language, is getting rid of or excising all of the traditional elements that you've learned as a writer.

AV: There are a couple of things for me to say here.

One of the reasons that I've been going to these megalithic sites in Europe is that there are so many of them. And some of them are vast. They are just vast—literally thousands of megaliths in Brittany, all in a single configuration, with other configurations nearby that are affiliated and they are connected to particular landscapes. They're enigmas. There's no language for understanding or clarifying why they exist, what they're there for. There's no written documentation for that. And one of the things in modernity that's happened—and this is why I think your work on Aboriginal landscape is so important—is we have not only forgotten, we've actively ignored the existence of all of these megaliths in Europe, in the UK, in Ireland, Scotland, but really even beyond that across the entire land mass all the way to East Asia. These things exist, and yet we act as if they have nothing to say to us. One of the reasons that your experience with Aborigines is so important is that in my estimation there you have a living culture that chose or saw the connections between the petroglyphs, the landscape, and the stories that go with them. And I wondered if you could say a little bit more about that because it's not just there are petroglyphs, it's that there are petroglyphs only in certain places. There are stories that connect only to a particular place and so there's this relationship between the human and the natural world and the spiritual world that are connected through literature, through story.

JC: I think the work that has to be done is to redefine those sacred sites, because we're only now talking about the fact that they exist, and ten years ago we probably wouldn't have. In other words, we've reached a point of understanding that we wouldn't have had in the past because we didn't know enough about these formations to believe that they actually had a story to talk back to us. That I've understood for a long time really because of my good fortune of being with Aborigines, but I think the link between the stationary megalith and the portable megalith needs to be recognized too so that in that Aboriginal culture, the portable megalith was the churinga—the stone storyboard. And these churingas I've always been fascinated with. In fact, I've written a couple of essays on the churinga. I mentioned it—I wrote about it I think in *Aboriginal Dreaming* just specifically about the churinga, because the churinga is a stone, a handheld megalith, and to penetrate that is a part of helping one to understand the larger formation or whatever that's not necessarily known about because the stories have been gone, but if you can get an Aborigine to read a churinga, he does it too in a way that's completely different than what we experience—knowledge past. It's done through the fingertips. Hapticism. They don't actually look at an object like a churinga and read it as you and I would read it, but the ancients could because they put the markings there. They actually have to put their fingers on it and so the story is expressed through the fingers—through the body.

AV: So they're reading the stone through another kind of perception, it's not through the visual alone as one may think, but it's rather through a direct perception where haptically, by touching, there's a kind of transmission. That is exactly what I'm talking about with regard to stones in, say, Ireland. Now, what I said was not entirely true about Ireland and Irish stones in that at different sacred sites in Ireland we do have stories. In that case, there are folk stories, legends and myths that have been conveyed and I'll give an example of that. Within about an hour of Dublin, there's a lake and there's a cairn and there are stones that are associated with the Cailleach—she is a hag who in the stories, carried the stones—she's associated with the lake and there are many stories about her, myths, really. The story of the cairns is that she was leaping from mountain to mountain with all of these stones in her apron and she would deposit them as cairns. There are other stories about her relations with a hero and his hair turning white. And he (or rather his men) has to negotiate to recover his vitality. There are stories like this about her, and the southwest part of Ireland is directly associated with her. These stories exist and they are associated with particular places and particular areas. She has sisters. They are associated with specific peninsulas. All of this is part of a kind of network that manifests on the landscape, but the experience comes in a couple of different ways and one of them I think is through—as you say, touching. Directly being there, touching stones—

JC: Kissing them?

AV: No. [laughs] Being open to what's there. What I've experienced on occasion is numinosity in the sense you're talking about, when you want to move the tent. I totally understand that, because I've had experiences which cross over into revelation of a kind of force or power you could say that is terrifying. It's beyond the human. It's direct contact with something that is beyond the human and that's what these stories are expressing. They can be read as children's stories that are purely amusing, but actually even children's stories are not that way if you look at the ancient stories. There are elements of what's terrifying in some of those ancient stories, so there's a crossover between awe and terror.

JC: Yes there is.

AV: And experience of the numinosity, because it goes beyond what we can normally assimilate.

JC: I agree with that and in the context of Aboriginal life, they actually identify this numen as what they call djang. But djang is something that they would say to you—over there is the manu rock, this is in the far Northwest. They say we shouldn't go too close to it unless we're initiated into it and we can sing the songs and ask permission because that rock has got djang in it, which is this gnosis. I remember it well, the cave in Arnhem Land where I went to see this great snake and witnessed it. Then the old men took me in; we stood back maybe fifty or sixty feet from this huge megalith. It's in [my book] *Sacred Places*, by the way. They would go along the entire snake with their hands, maybe forty feet of the snake. And as they went along the snake, they sang it up with words and then at the end, they asked permission of the snake for us to be there. We were okay being there, we're nice fellows and all, and so there was a whole ritual associated with it, but it all came through the fingers. The numen is in that embodiment of that painting; it's an icon of course.

AV: And it's in the rock too, that's the thing. It's not only the painting, it's the rock—the landscape itself is infused with it—it manifests.

JC: The other thing about it, because many of those Aboriginal myths—and I think probably most myths —are senseless. They make no sense.

AV: At the rational level.

JC: Yes, but we struggle to make them rational, therefore we make them into stories—folktales, whatever the logic behind creating Grimm's fairytales and other great composers of stories. They end up making folk experience out of it. They do it with Aboriginal stories too, but they've lost everything in the process because they're being made into objects of logic. And so for me, when I realized that you didn't have to understand a myth and that it had no logical outcome, then you settled into a different mode of experience with the myth. And it was therefore understandable when an Aborigine—I can remember for example, another good example, one day I went down into the desert with a man named Mick Tjakamarra, and I said, "Come on Mick, let's go out and have a cup of tea in the desert," and he said, "Oh, I'd love to do that" (because I'm [James was] a Tjakamarra too) and we were driving across a very deserted landscape, really arid and nothing growing. And he says stop here, Tjakamarra. I asked why would I stop here or anywhere? It wasn't particularly attractive. It wasn't a nice place with a bit shade or a dry river course. He said "No, no, stop here." He said there's a story up there and he got out of the car and I walked around the other side and there he was sitting on the ground already. He had taken out his cigarette tin and he started to tap out with his fingernails—long fingernails on the tin—a song. I asked, "How did you know it was here?" He said, "Oh, because I know this landscape like this here—I know where the songs are and I know when I can get out of the car and sing up that particular song." Can you imagine the power?—suddenly when I was looking at the landscape, it seemed to be rather arid and nondescript. Then came the embodiment of not only language, of story - it wasn't a logical story. He did translate it for me, but it made no sense. Two men, they come here, they make a fire, it makes no sense. That's the story. It's got no logic to it, it's just a part of the process and so when you realize that you're dealing with story in a much more dynamic way entering into landscape with an old man that sings up a song—it doesn't get any better than that, because you're actually in the place where myth emerges. So that's what I've experienced with great excitement and insight when I was with these old men, and that might help you in that endeavor to renew the contact between the megalith and you and the environment—the land underneath it, because it's the land underneath it too. It's the whole sense of an arid landscape or a tropical landscape—all those stories built it. When I was in Toraja many years later, I went there to re-establish a link with the myth that I had discovered about the heavenly letter. It was a very strange place, Toraja. Behind it all was this myth of the heavenly letter. It's nominally Christian, but ultimately what we're talking about is primal, mythological. So when I went there, and I eventually established my bearings and I got myself a guide—a young man that spoke English. I said these are the places I want to go and he said how would you know about these places? And I said because I've done some research on them. And when we went to these places and met the translator—the custodian if you'd like—they would tell me the myth of that place that we're in, but where they've fallen down was that they hadn't linked it to the village ten kilometers away who had a part of the myth too. So when I said to the old man—well, why don't we join the myths up, and we join the third one and the fourth one and we've got the whole myth of the holy family in front of us? And he said, we've never thought of doing that. So it was an interesting thing that evidently, they'd lost that common knowledge of the myth on the landscape and therefore were surprised that this writer would come in and advise them to share one another's stories much more, so as to actualize the myth. So that was another aspect of this story about Tjakamarra singing the song, to which I contributed by bringing them together.

AV: That's another aspect of this. There's a British writer, John Michell, who spent much of his life working on British sacred sites and connections between them and what I've observed and experienced is connected to that. He had particular perspective about what he called ley lines, which come from an earlier line of thinking.

JC: Old straight track.

AV: Old straight track and connections across the landscape, and that's analogous to what I'm talking about here, but it's directly related to what you're referring to, which is that a particular cairn, for example, at the top of a mountain in Ireland, can be seen on its own. It has its own astronomical, or astrological as the case may be, associations with stars, with the moon, with the sun, orientation in a particular direction that's connected to the movement of the stars, planets, to the landscape around it, but there are also places—megalithic sites—that are clearly connected as part of a larger pattern and some of them have stories connected or myths connected to them, but we tend to see them as individual, so you have on top of a hill here or over here a megalithic complex that has a story about it, but nearby are three others or ten others and we don't see that they're actually connected—they are connecting the landscape, and connected by aspects of the landscape, so there are larger patterns that are embedded into the landscape itself and the reason I think that's so important is that in the modern world we tend to see the land as objectified and divorced of and without any spiritual significance. But what these stories do and what you're talking about when your Aboriginal friend says stop here, there's a story. There's a story embedded in the landscape, and that story exists in what we can call an otherworldly sense in that it exists in a timeless way so that traveling through, he can access it. It exists outside time the way we think of it and in going past it, it's right there for him because it's not entirely in time the way we think of it. And what I'm saying is that at these megalithic sites, and this is true elsewhere as well, when you're there and you're open to it, what you're open to is in time and out of time. I mean the stones exist in time, but the stones also exist and carry something that's not entirely in time.

JC: Absolutely.

AV: And that's another matter entirely. In order to begin to even think about that, you'd have to let our modern kind of rationalistic materialistic expectations and conditioning—conditioning is a good word—you have to just drop it and accept that there are other ways of knowledge. That's okay. That's one mode of knowledge, but there are other modes of knowledge, and your story is beautiful about your Aboriginal friend who could access that. We can access that too. That's the thing. It's not completely outside our capacity to do it. It's not only him that can do it. I'm not saying we can access his Aboriginal story, but there are places where we can go and we can access stories too.

JC: And I think that again, it goes back to the issue of how story in landscape is expressed. We're accustomed to black on white on a page because of our literate culture, but when you bump up against people who are living oral culture, they have sophisticated methods of expressing things that we, as you rightly pointed out, in a sense have to re-learn as language, because it's a language we've had in an inherited sense, but it's not a language we consciously make available to ourselves. This is what we're really dealing with now is linguistically, is it possible to bring back to life this kind of thinking? Not necessarily the object itself, and we can get the story, yes, very interesting—but we're talking about something much deeper, more important about the whole human condition is that if we can find a way to reattach ourselves to that great inheritance that's preliterate and make it in a sense not post-literate, but you know what I'm getting at. In a sense, it's entering into a new language structure that we as writers have to embrace too. We have to—even to the extent of looking at the way we use a verb, or a noun, or an adjective, or an adverb, or a predicate, or a subject—these things have to be really looked at, because one of the other aspects of that sort of thing is you just say the landscape is a story. There is a megalith there. I understand it to the extent that it's related to me, but what is embedded in that story that's not available to me that may be available to that Aborigine? And then I look at his language and I've got books on various languages. I cannot speak the language of the Aborigines, but I can see it on the page and I can see when it's literally translated word for word. Firstly, it makes no sense until you really unscramble it. But secondly, you're looking at the way they put the important things to them into the sentence, so most important thing to us was "I." They didn't have an I, so once the psychology of "I" is removed from the story, you're already in a different perspective in terms of the way the mind thinks and that's the difficult thing, to shed the "I" into the non-I experience of a native Australian or Native American or even those Asian cultures, maybe the Native Americans had a sense of "I," I don't know. So it goes back to a linguistic environment too, to look at the language in which this myth comes out of and says oh, right, okay. I'm learning a little bit, I'm not learning a lot. You just keep playing with the ideas. But that's another area I thought was important to really experience this kind of landscape is through words in their language. Makes sense? I'm sure it does.

AV: What's the role of poetry and fiction with regard to what we're talking about? For the most part, the word "myth" has become synonymous with untruth, useless, lie. It's synonymous with those kinds of words, which is ridiculous. It's totally absurd, but that's our contemporary situation. And so somebody like Mircea Eliade whom we've both been reading—the Romanian historian of religion—most people aren't aware that he wrote fiction and his fiction was meant in part to convey in a modern context a very ancient perspective that's much more open to the numinous, and that's why his stories were often surreal, so people say—they use that term and of course surrealism was a contemporary movement fairly close to when he was writing. Also the stories and novels and novellas, written over his lifetime, were not completely historically contiguous. He's an example of someone who in my estimation, was clearly open to the other world. Really, that's what his novels, his novellas, his stories, were about. If you want to succinctly describe what he's doing, he's writing about what are really symbolic revelations of the other world in this world, which he called hierophanic.

JC: Beautiful word too.

AV: It is a beautiful word and I wondered what the relationship is between what we're talking about, which is working with the prehistoric, which is really what you've been doing with the Aborigines. What's the relationship between that and literature as we think about it today in contemporary literature?

JC: I think that contemporary literature is embroiled in the survival of the realist mode of thinking and therefore, it's desperate to hold onto a certain kind of fictional reality that is largely grounded in what we see and what we do and how we do it and the image of itself—whereas the kind of literature I'm talking about now has actually dispensed with that as the principal white screen, so to speak and put it behind it all, yet maintains some kind of relationship with it, and I call this in my language, metaphysical realism. What's happening in the real sense in the book is this metaphysic, but behind it is the realist mode that you've set it in, yet it's in no way determined by history. It's just you fixed on a point like I did in the trilogy in the thirteenth century in Spain in an inn. That's the realist backdrop and occasionally, I put in the props of a glass of wine and a beer and a meal just to keep the sense of reality there, but I'm not really writing it on that level. I'm not really writing at that level, but rather the metaphysical level and that's the level that I think fiction has yet to publicly announce itself to us. I think there are a number of writers who are very close to all that—I've been close. Others too, I think, are struggling to find a language to express a landscape outside the mode of the contemporary norm and the contemporary norm has no longer really the capacity to handle this material because it's grounded in realism. Grounded in secularism. It no longer partakes on the level of *Gawain and the Green Knight*, for example, which is a metaphysical tale but they'll pick that up and make it into a popular movie, as they did with *Star Wars* or one of those films, because the ideas had a surface value, but the real metaphysics is gone. I'm trying to reintroduce that metaphysics. I think that's what a writer must do—it doesn't matter whether you're never published again, you have to do it.

AV: Another way to talk about this—or to think about it—is that what you're calling realism is essentially the expression in literature of what in science is sometimes called materialism or scientism, meaning a kind of restriction—a self-imposed restriction of subject-object division, so there's a subject who is looking at an object—a glass of wine or a cup of coffee or whatever, and in science, the object is something one analyzes and perhaps performs an experiment on, and in literature, it's analogous to that in the sense that what you're talking about in terms of realism is division of subject and object and objectification of the small R—"realistic world." And with regard to science, simple dualism has been obliterated for the most part by quantum mechanics and quantum theories and also quantum discoveries that have emerged within the last twenty or thirty years and as verifying some aspects of quantum theories, actually completely obliterate materialist dualism in terms of how we understand science. So there's a division between that and what many scientists today espouse, which still derives from seventeenth-century or eighteenth-century simple dualism, a simple kind of objectification. But that dualist, materialist model doesn't work anymore. And yet many people, including physicists, continue this perspective and don't really take into account the sometimes alarming or certainly dramatically different ways of understanding that you see in the quantum world, and actually what I think you're talking about in terms of literature is comparable. The reason I say it's comparable is because on the one hand, we have a widespread literary realism that's analogous to a kind of simplistic Cartesian dualism. That doesn't hold anymore. It doesn't work. It can work as kind of a simple entertainment perhaps or even experimentation with words, but what's missing is what you're talking about in terms of the preliterate—the prehistoric—the archaic. I'm very fond of the word "archaic," and by archaic in this usage, I'm also referring to the sublime—the archaic in the sense of archetypical transcendence, the sublime, that which goes beyond subject-object dualism. And just as in quantum physics, it ultimately became necessary to leave behind some assumptions, so too, in terms of what we're talking about in literature, it's necessary to drop some of the assumptions that we come to literature with—maybe the way of doing that is going back to origins. And that's what you were doing with and are doing by going to Aboriginal cultures and Australian Aboriginal culture as you experienced it, going back to origins. It's experiencing origin of myth in the landscape—the living origin of myth and that is how metaphysical realism connects. That's where it comes from.

JC: You're quite right, and the word "origin" often used to pop up in my mind when I was working—is that you are actually going back to origins. At one level, you say this is absurd. This is a useless kind of nostalgia, but at another level I say no it's not, because actually the meaninglessness of life has been subsumed by the meaning that I'm receiving from this metaphysic so I think you've got to go with what's worthwhile. And you were absolutely right that the language of modern fiction is so grounded in the small r "real" that it's now perpetuated its own cliché. There's nothing of true value about modern literature from the latest Nobel prize winner through to the average costume novelist who writes about nostalgic history. Everything about the world in which they work is an absolute literary cliché. Not even to the point where they break the linear markings of the sentence on the page. They won't move away from that time sentence. Everything that happens in that sentence is going second by second by second and this is one of the things that I've been trying to break. People talk about my prose. They say it seems so vivid, it seems so timeless—even though it's embroiled in describing things that are in time. I work so hard to find the language on the page that broke with time. I was conscious of trying to break time because I learned from my experience with Aborigines that the myth was not in time. You made a very good point earlier that these sacred places, or these megaliths, are living in a zone of numinosity—and they're not everywhere as you rightly point out, because they are only in places where that dome of that many-colored glass, so to speak, is operating and therefore to penetrate it requires an act of humility. When you approach a sacred place or that dome, the only way through it, even though it's an invisible door, is through an act of humility. By entering into a space like that, humility pervades numinosity.

AV: It's the entry point—that's what permission means. You're asking permission. That, in itself is an act of humility. That is a point of entry and sometimes in these experiences you might be told yes, you can come back. That it's okay for you to come back. What that's saying is that there's recognition from the other side that on your side, you're open to the experience and to who is there, what is there.

JC: Let's talk about that, because that's important. You brought up earlier that the subject—and the verb that drives it and the object, which we live in, going into that thereness is no longer you as an "I" am going into an object and that's important. You've already started to break this linguistic prison by entering this space; what happens to you is we talked about humility, we talked about piety, but we didn't talk about—and I think this is part of it too—is abasement. You abase yourself in the presence of the numen where there is a megalithic site or a Chartres window. There is a certain element that we've forgotten because we now treat them as a secular object. When we walk into

Chartres we go in there as an object of history and observation—to see it, but we don't get in it as an act of abasement to the numen, which that is a perfect instructor of, it's a megalith, in a way.

AV: Chartres is on a megalithic site.

JC: It's on a megalithic site.

AV: On a sacred site that's much more ancient.

JC: Yes, but in a sense, it's another form of the megalith. It's just very visibly constructed in the way we understand construction, not like these people could see—they could see the mortar and the bricks of a cathedral if you'd like, in a rocky outcrop. In other words, they filled in the gaps that we don't do anymore. We actually objectify it by putting a roof on it and things like that and we say well we've got a sacred site. The ancients didn't need to do that. They had the myth, which enveloped, as you say and placed it inside the numen and at the same time, filled it out almost physically, but certainly psychologically with form like Chartres cathedral and that is why these megalithic sites attract us, because we are still struggling to understand the form, but we know it's there and we're going to get to it because that's what we're tasked to do.

AV: There's another dimension or another aspect of what we're talking about that we haven't mentioned that I think is critical, and that is consciousness itself, because really what we're talking about is a kind of consciousness. I'd say the term "access" is not exactly right—I used that term earlier. It's a way to talk about it, but another term might be participation—that you can participate in the story or participate in the place itself and its story or what it conveys, but that comes through an act of consciousness and experience through consciousness, which is itself in some respects, timeless. Timeless meaning that what is carried in that particular place is not restricted to a particular generation or a particular person, but is something that we can participate in if we approach the place in a particular kind of way, which includes being humble—being humbled, you're right, the word doesn't really fully express because really what we're talking about is selflessness—a moment in which self to a greater or lesser extent, vanishes. There's also an element, which I want to bring in, which is the reason I brought in terror or awe, is that so many of these megaliths and cairns are largely untouched. People are a little frightened of them, and do not go around them for the most part. They don't go looking for them. A few modern pagans will show up and leave something or other there, an offering some kind. The reason that the local people don't mess with these places is that they're a little scared of them and that's with good reason. Because what we're talking about is beyond this self-other dichotomy. We assume that there is a self, which is imagined as hard, opaque, unchanging on the one side and on the other side are objects and they're completely separated, whereas one of the alarming things about these stories is that—in the sacred places—that's not actually how it is. We participate in the place and there's some amount of risk in that. It's a risk to the hard-opaque self and to what we want to hold on to.

JC: I think it's interesting that you've alluded to three things. Awe, fear, or horror—or what was the word you used?

AV: Terror.

JC: Awe and terror—there are two words that have—firstly I'll just address them because I think they're interesting. These two words actually jolt us out of the context of being who we are, and that is because something is pressed upon us, revealing a greater power, and so we feel terror and we feel awe. The trouble within the modern context is we see those words associated with a loss of life, but that's not what the ancients really meant.

AV: Not necessarily.

JC: No they might've felt that they might be killed by the power of the place, but ultimately the awe and the terror was about the extraordinary nature of the numen that was before them, and if it killed them, that was a byproduct of the issue, but it was not the normal fear of saying "God, there's a crocodile that's going to take me." That's what I'm trying to say and so those two words and abasement and humility are part of that—then you brought up the idea of time. And it struck me that the issue of time is removed as you rightly point out, by the act of humility and abasement and terror and awe, but suddenly we're captured by the whole context of time, which for us in the modern world, we have been embroiled. We're caught in time, but we don't know a way out of it. Clearly people like Aborigines do know a way out of it because their sense of the "I" doesn't exist the way ours does. I used to say to Wendy that Aborigines had no personality, but they're full of character because personality is a projection of yourself whereas character is a projection of the other in a collective sense, so the Aborigines really engaged in a relationship with somebody else and so they don't have the personality that we see as reality. Time is removed when you are not walking around in space, so to speak because you've got no "I." And that is where these places become so powerful. They may be invisible constructs of timelessness or eternity on landscape. Does that make any sense to you?

AV: It does, it does make sense. I think that's a beautiful way to put it. Timeless manifestations—manifestations of timelessness in landscape.

JC: Yes, and that's where you're moving towards when you originally remarked upon the fact that there were vast places full of these extraordinary stones in groups here and groups there, it was—you say well there's numinosity over there, there's numinosity here, there's a set of stories perhaps in landscape and that's what we were discussing earlier with regard to the special relationship between these and yourself. And so when we go back—and I'm just pursuing a little bit further, the idea that language has got something to do with it. We have frozen our language to the point where it's very good at doing what it does—it can beautifully express in science, the cliché of certain things in the novel and language generally, but we've lost the grounding upon which language sits—language emerges from something, and my belief now is that language emerges from the earth. It's not just a facile construct of the human mind. It's part of that osmotic process between the human being's emerging consciousness and the earth. It's always a gauge of the nexus there, and language was the first way that came into being. I'm saying we shouldn't separate language off into something that we made because once you do that, you're already enervating yourself to the point where you say well with language, I am a superior being. I can understand and analyze landscape and so forth. So my sense is that when a man sits on the ground and says there's a song in the earth, he's basically saying this piece of land is linguistically recognizable to me. It's talking to me and that is the quality that I'm trying to find and I won't ever achieve it, but I expect you to—is how do you get that relationship between earth, the terranean existence, if you like, numen, and the lingual process as it appears on the page? That is the long and difficult trace that you have to take on now because you're already alerted to the fact that language as we know it is a frozen species and you—we as writers—have to break that. We're the only ones—we're the scientists of language. It's not the semioticians and people studying in academe, it's the writer who always breaks down and makes language new again.

AV: And what you're referring to by going to origins

is—going back to origins is this connection between landscape and language and the spiritual or other world. And we're the conduit for that.

JC: Yes.

AV: One part of that is also the image—stones can speak in images or be conveyors of images, sometimes in terms of petroglyphs, but sometimes not. Petroglyphs are an expression through image, but sometimes images can be conveyed without being visible to the eye. That's part of the song that you're talking about with your friend who was an Aborigine—he may have been able to see images as it were embedded in the earth itself or manifesting there and that those images are connections between us and—or him and so on, perhaps 200, perhaps 2,000 or 3,000 or 5,000 years ago.

JC: Or an eternity.

AV: Those images are in eternity as it were and thinking about writing in the light of timelessness is what we're really talking about, the expression of timelessness, because that's what those megaliths are. They are expressions of timelessness in time in a particular landscape and so is writing.

JC: That's right and that's the issue of deconstruction of the modern language to make it timeless again. That is the task. It's finding that way back to the way an adjective, a noun, and a verb worked in origin—*ab origine*. That's where studying those old languages, even though you don't necessarily understand them *in toto*, you acknowledge—

AV:—Or you may.

JC:—You may, but it's a tough ask. I wish I could've at twenty learned an Aboriginal language, but once you get into the understanding that that language is an entirely different construct, it's placing psychology in a different place altogether in terms of the sentence. Then you are starting to prepare yourself to break with the constraints of present-day language and go back, because it's in the earth, you see, and re-establish that link if you'd like with the terrene existence—I feel I will read a new language. It wouldn't happen in my lifetime, but it one day will be seen as being as revolutionary as some of the other ones, like Joyce when Joyce wrote stream of consciousness. That was a break with the past in the terms of linguistic identity of character on page. Gertrude Stein made some very remarkable breaks with language. That sort of change hasn't been seen since Beckett.

AV: The difference between what you're alluding to—modernist efforts at essentially experimentation with language—is different than what we're talking about here, I think. What we're discussing, we can call metaphysical realism or metaphysical literature more broadly. Because it emerges out of conscious participation in and expression of timelessness in time through symbol, through story, through poetic expression. And that's new. It's very, very old. It's the new archaic. It's the archaic made new and without that you can't have ultimately renewal. It's a manifestation of new culture manifesting in its purest form—that's the beginning—the stories, the songs. That's the manifestation of them at the very beginning anew and that's essentially where we are today is—

JC:—on the cusp—

AV:—both at the end of it—the end of culture and in culture at risk of complete dissolution, certainly in Europe. I think that's undeniable. And yet, at the same time, at the cusp of renewal. That renewal requires return to origins in a very profound way and I think that might be an extremely interesting point to close it.

JC: That cusp that you talk about and that return to origin is really embodied in the Ouroboros.

Second Conversation:

FREEDOM

AV: Yesterday we discussed language in relation to the archaic and the transition from prehistoric to historical. We discussed the uses of language within the historical era, how to read the archaic, and the idea of megaliths as manifestations within a landscape. And we started to talk a bit about—or at least allude to—the transition between language of stone and written language. And there's an intermediary, which is the language of image. What I thought we might start to explore is that transition, which is embodied in images like spirals and wavy lines.

JC: Celtic knots.

AV: Celtic knots. Those kind of images that appear on petroglyphs or in the Australian context, churingas. That's a kind of transition, you could say, because a churinga has a symbolic language on it, but then it's read in a sort of mysterious way. It's not read—you'd say that it's "rcad."

JC: Yes, that's a valid point, since the transmission of image is expressed through fingers. Because in the end, the images made by fingers are coming out of a mental construct. The image is pre-imagined before it's constructed, and that link between the imagined image and the image on the churinga, say, is one of the great mysteries, because we don't know whether the image that is pre-imagined is an image that the auditor has received from a tree, from bark, from a spiral. When a tree is cut, you see certain images. My sense is that that's probably true—that nature has gifted the pre-image, and that the image we see that's not in a language or not in text is in that transitional phase from, say, the tree to the image in the mind of the auditor to his translation of that with his fingers and his artifacts to a latter stage, which becomes phonetics and language. It's a long linear line but language is ultimately the inheritor of a natural disposition.

AV: The language of nature.

JC: That's right.

AV: Because what we're really talking about is a language of nature in the Pythagorean-Platonic sense to some degree, but also anterior to that. It's more archaic than that. It is more from the era of the shamanic, because of course Pythagoreanism and Platonism are very rarely discussed except among scholars, but the consensus is that they come out of those archaic traditions. Those high Greek traditions come out of shamanism and shamanism is contact with the truly archaic and with the language of nature in itself. And so a churinga, which is an oblong piece of stone or of wood that's got the symbolic images in it—what you're saying is that those images are the language of nature anterior to written language and in a sense, were more immediate because by touching the image through the haptic, you're accessing the Aboriginal individual accessing that—that language of nature itself from a particular place. Particular landscape.

JC: I agree with that. I would say that the haptic experience is probably a pre—I hesitate to use the world intellectualize, but it's a pre-conceiving way of absorbing knowledge. So pre—

AV: Pre-conceptual.

JC: Yes, preconceptual is what I mean. Our knowledge is entirely conceptual. Whatever we do, we pay lip service to nature at a certain level, but ultimately, we receive all of our information conceptually. There was a time when humankind didn't. And this is the time when you touch something and you receive knowledge through your fingers because this in a sense predates the conceptual mind by millennia. That's my sense of things. That's how nature imposes itself on humankind.

AV: And so to put it perhaps a bit elliptically, it's possible to touch an object and to be able to "read" it, by which one means directly access through that haptic moment. Images or stories or the landscape itself and its mythological dimension, which is preconceptual, or it's non-conceptual. It's not a set of concepts about the landscape, it's the actual landscape and the myths—the stories that are embedded in it—directly accessed.

JC: I agree with that totally. I think that that's then lending itself to that concept of origin. You're getting very close to origin when you start to think or talk or feel or touch in this dimension. Because you know you've already shut out preconception, conception, intellectualization, text—all of the things that we take for granted are gone. They've been removed from this process and so in a way, returning to origin through object is a clarification of the way we have seen in the past. We've lost the seeing-ness in our time, but we are trying to regain it without necessarily going back into a nostalgic environment because we're not doing that, but we're trying to find something that was lost, and we want to regain it. And that's really a platonic concept anyway, because he would argue that everything is known. In a sense, we've forgotten it.

AV: Anamnesis.

JC: Yes, anamnesis. And we are struggling to break that veil if you like and come through it. And of course it's not easy because we've no tools really, except intuition.

AV: We have intuition, but intuition is enough. Where we are, I think today in the contemporary world is, in terms of the writer's life, a kind of bifurcation. On the one side we have analytical, conceptually driven kinds of non-fiction writing typically. Or fiction, which is often either realistic or fantastic, but not necessarily reflecting or connected to this kind of knowing we're referring to here, and that's something that we've talked about individually before. I wondered what you might have to say about what you call metaphysical realism, and how the literature you've written corresponds to going beyond either on the one hand purely analytical kinds of prose, or on the other hand, either fantastic in the sense of fantasy or strictly realistic literature. How does metaphysical realism correspond to what we're talking about?

JC: I think that you have to actually examine what metaphysics means, firstly. And acknowledge that it means in a literal sense, beyond physics. So it's beyond the physical and therefore in a sense, immaterial, as a concept and as a way forward in a thinking process. And so to apply that to a literary genre requires from you to examine the kind of metaphors that you are projecting on the page so that these metaphors become automatically elliptic. They are automatically charged with metaphysic. And it's not only the individual word that's charged with metaphysic. It's the sentence and then the paragraph so you're actually building up a set of metaphors and images that convey a story within a story. The esoterism of the narrative, if you like. And it's very hard to define that new language or that old language because it's an old language too. Arthurian legendary tales of the twelfth and thirteenth century are wonderful examples—the Arthurian stories are characteristic of this in the European tradition, and my sense is that if you can get a metaphysical reality working properly, it means that you backdrop the narrative that you are trying to express with a kind of pseudo-realism. It's not a real realism. You set your novel in a certain kind of place or time, but you acknowledge already that that time and place are debunked. You've just set them there like a prop for something else that's going to happen within the narrative and that's the metaphysic and the language that you're going to use there is entirely driven by a certain sense that the other world, namely the possibility of a human being—being always in the other world when he speaks—he can therefore express a metaphysic in the ordinary when he articulates on the page. That's the difficult area, and my experience with it over the years now is that if you can find a way to acknowledge the power of intuition as a literary device rather than just a human device, just separate those two—they're linked of course, but we, in a general sense, use intuition as some kind of foreknowledge or kind of sense of things going on around you that you've picked up on. But in the literary process what you're doing intuitionally is abandoning realism consciously in the sentence when your character begins to talk, or when you describe a certain activity on the page. Realism is abandoned—the categories are abandoned—intuition comes into ultimate play, and then you start to find a disjoint between time and place. You can allow your characters then to enter multiple time and multiple place even though in the illusion of the backdrop, they are somehow situated in time. And particularly when I did the first book—*Snow on the Camino Real*—I introduced there probably for the first time in many, many, many years, a genuine spirit in the character of Hakekit ibn al-Hayut, the character that inspired my Abu Said al-

Hassan who was the figure that appeared out of the night so to speak on the river as a young man and so got to talking to him and said, "I come from no place, and I expect you"—and of course it changed his life and he decided go on the metaphysical journey. From then on, his whole life he was a philosopher. And in that character Hakekit ibn al-Hayut, I thought to myself how can I, in twenty-first-century literature, introduce a genuine spirit into a manuscript that constantly turns up like a trickster hero right throughout the text? And make it in a sense, real for the reader because he has to approach and accept Hakekit ibn al-Hayut as a figure in the book? And it was in the process of redrafting, and redrafting in particular *Snow in the Camino Real*, because that was the hardest, to get that language going. The character Hakekit finally emphasized himself to the point where he was one of the characters in the book and he was in a sense a human, but he was also utterly human and he was spirit. And he goes through the whole three of these books. But that's the metaphysical realist approach that you can suddenly find a way to once more do what Homer did when Odysseus arrives on the reef and meets Ino there, the Goddess, and she guides him onto the place where he goes. I always found that fascinating—the fluidity of the Gods in Greek epic. I don't see them [as Gods] at all, but as abstract metaphysical elements within the context of literature and they work seamlessly and that's what I feel that new literature must go back to. That sense of the other—the integral to you as a human being or as a character in the current age.

AV: A collection of words, all related, that I think are helpful here is derived from hieros and includes hieratic, hierophant, hierophantic and so forth. Having to do with the revelation in the quotidian of what transcends the quotidian, because as Eliade said, the sacred is revealed in the profane. That's —

JC: That's what metaphysical realism is, really.

AV: That's what it is. The sacred is revealed in the profane, and so what you're referring to is a hieratic event or a hieratic dialogue, and you've alluded to the novel *Troubadour's Testament* as being an example of that. So that was the first instance in which you were really exploring the hieratic and I wondered if you could explore that a little more.

JC: That was a very interesting time to be writing a book. I felt it was important to link up the past with the present through the death roll, and the death roll in a sense created the illusion of time conflated or compressed. I wanted that sense—that time could have an immediate presence in the present and the only way to do it was through this tracing backwards—this death roll [a manuscript] to its origin. He didn't follow it from its birthplace in the mountains and that was deliberate—to its end place. He picked up at the end place and he followed it back in order to figure out why the manuscript ended up in the river. It was because the poet himself felt that language had failed him, so he threw it away. He abandoned language and that was the critical aspect of Marcebru, the character of the Troubadour poet—he finally realized that he'd been trying to gain approval through other people's voices by way of the death roll for the justification for the love of the woman that he met and had passed away, and why had she died. And in the end, he couldn't answer the question, so he threw away the manuscript, acknowledging he failed. And the allusion there was to the fact that in the twentieth century when I wrote it, language was failing us. We were throwing it in the river. There was nowhere to go. And so when I started writing that book, I said I can't people it as I might've earlier books—particularly the books like *Messengers of the Gods*—with real people. I had to actually remove myself entirely from real people and construct angelic entities who in fact were particularly described in the book—one wears a blue shirt, one walks in a certain kind of way, and the other lives in the house of —, and he's a member of one tariqa and dresses up in Arabic gear. And the fellow that was selling fine quality paper, and he tells the narrator look through the paper. Don't see the surface of things. Inside there is an amulet. That amulet belongs to the Bogomils—another metaphysic presented on paper—and that's what I sell to you. So each of the characters throughout that book represent and manifest themselves as angelic entities to the narrator who is slowly of course going back to discover the history of the death roll and so also goes deep in himself, and he's returned to origin and so the people he meets become more and more profound as he goes along backwards through that journey through Troubadour to the point where he finally seeks the revelation of the death of Amedée de Jois, her name means "Amedée of joy." She's an allegorical character really, but she's based on realism. You've seen a photograph of her. That's the sort of the thing that as a writer I think today, you're working with much more than just "Oh well, I can set up a plot. I can get a few characters going. I've got time: fill sentences. Off I go. I can talk about the hill. I can talk about the car. I can turn around, have my characters doing all of this." They're all the props of an antique form of writing. To make props that are surreal is the hardest thing to do, and you have to find a way and I think in *Troubadour*, that's where I started the process, and it only matured in those later books.

AV: Hieratic language might be expressed in a way that's stylized or in a manifestation that to some extent either signals or pulls you out of a strictly realistic mold, so in some sense, it's at odds with a kind of materialistic and limited view of the world. What that means is that the language of characters is merged with a language of the metaphors that you're using. The language itself is simultaneously drawing in, but also in some sense, pulling beyond through that tension. And symbolically evoking or in some sense, manifesting what's embedded in the text as it were. And that's pointing beyond itself.

JC: Yes, yes, and that is such a rare quality for us to identify with in this day and age because we're so immune to it. We're immune to it. We're being debted with another form of expression, but if you read the ancient epics and you read the early medieval allegories, you'll mainly know that you're being confronted by another language and initially you just say this is a bunch of gods on the page and they are silly and do silly things, because you are applying logic, the old-time modern logic to a set of parameters which are entirely metaphysical. The Gods of the Greeks, for example, are not illogical, bad-mannered, bad-tempered people in the sense that even the classicists would argue, claiming that basically they're a bunch of useless objects, the twelve Gods, because nobody has seen these Gods as pure metaphysic. And the fact that Homer or whoever wrote it could translate their pure metaphysic onto the page and have them seamlessly engage with humans is a language that in the twenty-first century—we look at askance. Doesn't mean anything to us, but as creative writers, we have to actually re-engage with that. That seamlessness. And in my lifetime, having been engaging with Aborigines and tribal peoples, that allowed me to realize that to get between thought and language should be seamless. Should be known, so if we talk about the Dreaming, it's the same as talking about I'm thinking about getting a kangaroo. There's no sort of a sense of a device between you, which is in our own language—thought and action and dualism, etc. They don't think like that. And that's why I went to tribal landscapes—to cleanse my language, not because I was interested in the exotic *per se*. I was more interested always in what we were talking about into—and in many cases when I talked to Aborigines or Torajins or people in the desert, it was always about language. They would say well what do you mean by that? Or I'd say what do you mean by that? And sometimes I came up against the wall—a tribal person would say, "Well, we don't have the language equipment to answer that question." Then I knew we were getting close. A long way back in terms of conceptualization to get there. I'm trying to get him to conceive or conceptualize. He's mystical. He's in a mystical environment—and he can't do it.

AV: Because what we're talking about is pre-conceptual. It is non-conceptual in the sense that the dreaming is present in the landscape itself. It's not that one has a conception that then is externally applied to it, but from the Aboriginal perspective, the landscape which includes water and all aspects of nature, is itself a manifestation of—and in some sense, indivisible from the Dreaming.

JC: That's right. And that inseparability is what we have lost today. We can't conceive of an inseparable relationship between the Dreaming, which is a mythologic expression of this world and the other world, which is embodied in nature because nature is both material and metaphysical. It came up today in our discussions: well, do you talk about nature as a physical thing—as a metaphysical thing? And the question was asked. I said well, it's clear they're both. But to talk about nature as a metaphysical entity is—well, it's impossible to talk about it that way. Scientists would just reduce you to nothing and tell you it's all about enzymes or whatever. But the Aborigine would look at that landscape and say it's entirely metaphysical. Every tree. Every *manu* stone. Every cave. Every rock formation is manifestly metaphysical. That—I think science will come to terms with it eventually because I think that they're already going into non-matter as a concept and realizing that matter is actually not what we think it is, and so my sense is that that aspect of nature is there in the past. It needs to be brought back into our world, and literature is probably the only way we can do it, at least initially.

AV: What literature does—what it can do in a contemporary context is provide a means for the reawakening and re-emergence of the mythical, and the mythical is another way of expressing what you're terming metaphysical reality.

JC: It's a tool.

AV: Yes, and the arts in general more broadly can do that but literature has a particular kind of role, because it's the telling of stories, of narratives that can in a unique way, convey this. And for us, in the modern world, this is hard to conceive of because for us, myth has become synonymous with falsehood. People talk about the myth of this, or the myth of—the myth of something else in a very dismissive way. It's a way of dismissing something as not real. And that concept "not real" is an almost exact mirror image—an inversion of what we're talking about because from a Platonic perspective, myth is actually referring to what is more real than the physical. And to some extent, of course quantum mechanics is disassembling the material as it were, showing us that our Cartesian and dualistic assumptions about the nature of the world around us and our relation to it are false. Quantum mechanics, different quantum theories have called that into question. But those only actually go so far and what literature does is something different. At its best, it's answering a deep need that we have to understand in more profoundly our relationship to the natural world, but also to what sometimes is called the other world. In Celtic tradition, it's referred to as the otherworld. You use that term as well. And that's embedded in Aboriginal traditions too because the Dreaming is a way of expressing metaphysical reality, meaning the metaphysical reality of not only this world, but of divine spiritual reality embedded in nature, through which we find human meaning and that is in part what you're working with, and also finding a new language to express in your novels in particular.

JC: True. Looking back too, I would say that in *Messengers of the Gods,* which was a nonfiction narrative in a sense, as well as a metaphysical tale. It was there I made the conscious decision that the myth has to be entered physically as well as intellectually. All right, it might be the wrong thing to do, but you've got to experiment. I'm still a scientist in a sense. I'm still playing with the concept that things are risky business, but you've got to test them as a theory. So when I did *Messengers*, I chose three different landscapes, a sea landscape, a forest landscape, and a desert landscape. All of which represented earth, sea and air, and I the writer was fire. So I looked at the journey as an alchemical journey within tribal constructs. And I wanted to enter the myth and meet the people that own the myth. So this was entirely different fiction where I was going to create characters that are in their own myth. Here I am meeting people who own the myth in the real sense and so getting into their lives and walking through a myth with them and walking along a beach and having somebody in Mer tell me the story of Malu, the great octopus or going to Borneo and talking about Sengalang Burong and the great kite. Or going to Kimberley and talking to an old Aboriginal in a cave telling a story about the Wandjina. I was encountering the physical natural myth that was sitting in the dirt in the cave and telling us a story—the old man is telling me a story underneath the great tree. I now realized that I had to find a way to bring the physical into the metaphysical and vice versa in literature. So I learned most of my early techniques and thoughts about metaphysical realism in that world before I even really took it on as a thing to do as a writer because I didn't know. I was learning from that rarified world of hierography, hiero-history and in a sense, hiero-geography. That these people living in an entirely metaphysical landscape made up of rivers and trees and forests and things and that and then that translated to stories. And that translated into churingas. That translated into whole compendium, a library of sacred knowledge, and that to me was the key that literature had forgotten—thrown over its shoulder and we had to get it back. And put it in the door and open it.

AV: And that idea of hiero-geography and hiero-history, meaning the history of hieratic journeys, of revelation through a particular landscape, is something that we share in terms of a natural approach to writing, meaning writing is the expression of that. When we are in a particular landscape, we explore, and by exploring, we're also coming to understand not only the landscape, but also its metaphysical dimensions simultaneously. One of the things that you find in the modern world is a kind of desacralized landscape and some people will argue that the idea of disenchantment and secularization is not real. Secularization didn't actually happen, they claim. But in fact it did happen, and objectively you can demonstrate that because what's happened is progressively, for example in Western Europe, the forgetting of the meaning of all of these sacred sites that people literally do not see. There are megaliths everywhere in Western Europe, which includes of course England, Ireland, Scotland, Wales, but also Brittany, Cornwall in particular, so you have this metaphysical landscape expressed in stone throughout Western Europe. Yet people have no idea, for the most part, that it's there. Then you have the overlay of Christianity on top of that, so you have great cathedrals built sometimes on top of, for instance, very clearly on top of sacred springs, sacred places within the Pagan tradition. There's a great cathedral built there, but those are depopulated now in the sense that statistically Christianity is very much on the wane in Western Europe. You have a little bit of resurgence of Paganism, but for the most part, not completely, I'm not saying completely, but for the most part, you have a lack of cognizance of the idea of a sacred landscape and that then also manifests itself in the lack of a sacred landscape in literature and that has—you could say metaphysical consequences all across the spectrum of human life because then we don't see nature. We don't see the natural world as sacred. We don't understand our relationship to it, and as a result, you have the kind of society developing that we see today. And so there's a larger set of implications to what we're discussing. But also regarding the effort to understand the ancient and the archaic in new ways in our contemporary world, it's in that context that our exploration of different sacred places and sacred contexts needs to be understood. I think in the modern world, we need to recover. We must recover a more coherent understanding of who we are, taking into account what has been lost, but is there to be recovered and understood in a new way. Now, when you're talking about the hieratic and hieratic characters, that has a particular kind of relation to literature because it's bringing literature back to a very ancient way of understanding where when you see a bird, that bird is a bird, but it also may be a spirit-being, another way of expressing an irruption into the profane of the sacred, so nothing in a novel or in non-fiction is necessarily outside the sacred in the context we're talking about.

JC: But its constraint of course is in the language that overlays it, which in the present day makes it difficult for it to irrupt because the irruption breaks conventions that are already firmly rooted in the psyche of the reader, so to speak. And so you as a writer have to find a way to break that and allow the irruption to happen so that the readers says "Oh yeah, I can take that." Instead of saying "No, I can't." There was an allusion made today by one of my friends, Len. He said to my friend Don, "You're reading James's work to him?" And Don said "Oh, yes. It's a remarkable experience to read the books to him," and meant it. Then he replied "And you understand what he's saying?" And Don turned around and said "Of course I understand what he's saying. It's so pure." He said, "When I leave this house, I'm more clear of mind. I come here for an injection of text of a very particular set of characters that are always bringing you up into the metaphysical." Now he's never experienced this before. He's a reader, but I said to his wife, Paula, "Oh my God, where did we go today? It was just tremendous." I go there too, because I'm listening. I'm not any more the writer, I'm just listening to something that I've written. And I think my God: where was I when I wrote that because there's no device in it? There's no sense of I'm going to try and get these characters onto another situation, have another sex scene or dadada. These characters determine their own metaphysic on the page that I'm receiving as a reader—a listener—like Don, and I realized then he goes down and does the reading for me once a week to these people because they want to know—they want to have that sense of walking out of there saying "I'm in another world." And that's what metaphysical realism—what literature—should be about. It was for the ancients. You walked out of a session of songsters or rhapsodists in ancient Greece and you were moved. If you weren't, then you were an impossible being—to hear Homer sung in a dark space or a light space by a fire had a powerful effect upon people, and if you can get 25,000 people in to listen to and watch a play—we can't do that, but they did it—not regularly, but when they did it, they did it because they were listening to the hieratic thrusts into this consciousness and exploding in terms of words, which goes back to nature and all that we talked about it earlier.

AV: That's right, and something that connects to that and I think is important to say, so I'm just going to say it, is that there's a connection here to the ancient Mysteries. The ancient Mysteries included mythological revelations in a particular setting. It's pre-theater. This exists before any concept of what we would today call theater, but rather you have revelation of hieratic text and image in this—often in a cave setting or inside a Mystery temple, for example Samothrace, Samothraki, an island off the coast of Greece, which was famous for more than 1,000 years as a Mystery center, and for the revelation, this kind of Mystery revelation. But what I want to say in connection to that is that what you're talking about is essentially a kind of Mystery dimension within the contemporary text and the Mysteries have an inside and an outside—there are those who really for whom the Mysteries are a closed book as it were. It's not necessarily for everyone. There were initiates, and there were people who were not initiated, and those who were initiated did not talk about their knowledge to those were not initiated into the Mysteries. So there's some sense in which the sacred, and this is true for Aborigines, can't necessarily be conveyed, so what we're doing is moving between what is esoteric and what is exoteric and there are those for whom what is exoteric is all there is and that's okay. That's okay. So what we're discussing is not necessarily for everyone. It's for those to whom it speaks.

JC: Yes, but I think the esoteric, if it's embedded in a text or a space or a work of art and has an exoteric dimension, which is the physical dimension, allowing us to see it or to hear it, necessarily is retained by the exoterist listening to it without his knowledge. The esoteric by its nature is fluid. It seeps into things—it has no barriers and it will enter the mind of an ordinary person without him knowing and will temper things without him knowing in his life, so it's not as though the esoteric is only there for those who understand and are conscious of its breakdown so to speak. My sense of the esoteric is that it imparts its esoterism into exoterism. Last night we watched an extraordinary movie where—going back to your earlier thoughts about the temple and the temple in the Mystery tradition—the Aborigines built a temple over a period of two and a half days.

AV: Yes, Australian Aborigines, in building a fire ceremony, they built a temple.

JC: They graded the ground. They put in a large painting. They went through the story. They created the nest of the Great Snake. They put up the world tree in two places on each end of that space. They put a barrier—remember the barrier or hedge all the way around the upright sticks to create the temple space. And there you were seeing in a sense a nomadic temple—a nomadic megalith being created for the ceremony. Then they—remember?—they knocked it all down and threw it all apart and said go home now. Pretend it never happened. That's why the film is so extraordinary, because it's taking you to a place that we've never been in terms of church architectures or Greek architecture, which is a sort of space constructed by minds. Here we've got the very Earth—paintings all over your body, the dirt, putting on all that red soil. You can see all the transformations going on there, but we take it for granted because they're Aborigines. They do silly things. But they are actually acting out a hierophany for three days. And all of those people are observing, and they're watching the figurative activity to the extent that they recognize he's making a mistake. This perfection in architecture of the human body dancing. He knows the way they should dance. Everybody hit the ground at exactly the same time and they're—all the dancing is from the hip down. That to me is extraordinary. In other words, the language of the Earth only goes as far as the hips and that's beautiful to me. And Native Americans do the same, they have this very strange footwork as they dance. It's all in the feet. It's not like Westerners, where it's all expressive through the arms. It is through the legs in ballet, too, but ultimately, it's about the whole body expressing itself, whereas for the Aborigines, what happens in their hands is a kind of appendage to this incredible language of legs. Coming out of the Earth, it's just like almost churingas. That's my sense of what a great ceremony and a great test of thought is, and it's that originary nature of communication that seems to me that literature has to regain. You can't dance on paper in the same way, but you can figuratively express the dance, whether it's a mind dance, whether it's a human dance, whether it's two people discussing a paper in a shop in an long-gone place, it's always about creating an intellectual freedom that is so powerful that when you walk out of that shop, the character, or whatever, or the reader walks out of the shop—he knows or she knows that I've come into contact with something that was ordinary, that's now transformative outside. That's metaphysical realism.

AV: But there is a distinction I think between those who know the dance—the fire ceremony—and recognize, as you say, the temenos, the sacred space, and those outside the sacred space. There are those who are initiated into the different skin groups, who are able to be more present than those who are not initiated. There is still outsider and insider as it were. And esoteric really in this context means being able to read—being able to see. Being able to understand what's happening. Being able to see the story and hear the story and participate in the story and have the story. And not everyone has that. And so there are people who look at that fire ceremony and say well that's exciting visually, I guess, or not. Or maybe boring or whatever, but it doesn't actually mean something.

JC: But the old men knew.

AV: The old men knew. There's an esoteric dimension to that fire ceremony.

JC: That's right. In my trilogy I talked about it as being that people could be divided into knowers or watchers. And the characters who were watchers were the ones who were talking about living exoterically. Absorb the information but can't translate it into a knowing and I think in one of the early chapters of *Prodigals*, Benjamin of Tudela meets a Jewish man who studies the Kabbala in Toledo in the early, early chapters and the catechist says yes, I know a lot about it, but I'm still only a watcher. I don't—I haven't had a genuine experience out of it, so hence I continue to study it. And so there are even those who were in so to speak the knowledgeable realm that are still exoterists. They are still outside the world of its essence like the Kabbalah, so I put that in there. And the second book that came out—the one you were talking about that Abu Said, who is the philosopher in this section of books, finally meets his match in the second novel in the trilogy, *The Prodigals.*

AV: What's called the Kingdoms trilogy of novels.

JC: Yes, the Kingdoms trilogy. He finally finds himself in jail in Mecca because he has been turned in because he's an iconoclast and he's a danger to Islam and so they throw him in jail—he's come home, but he ends up in jail, and when he wakes up—when he gets his eyes accustomed to the candle-light, he finds himself in this cell with a stonecutter from Basra, a pickpocketer who lives off the streets of Mecca stealing from people's pockets. But originally he was a stonecutter, and Abu Said, he is a great philosopher, who thinks "I'm stuck in a cell with a stonecutter who is a pickpocketer and we're totally at odds in life." But eventually this stonecutter enables him to get out of there, because he understands stone, and he's able to break through the wall during an earthquake—a minor earthquake in Mecca—and get out. But eventually he says well, you better stay with me and take me back—I've got a job to do in Persia, for I've got to write something on a slab of rock that was left by the great Persian—

AV: Xerxes.

JC: Xerxes, who had left one section of slab blank and Abu Said realizes he's going to have write something on that slab, and it's going to be the Book of Kingdoms, which is a text within the first book. And he asks the stonecutter to do the work, because he's the only one that can climb up on a rig and hang over the great slab and he will write—with Abu Said telling him the words to write out, so they had the combination of an intellect on the ground with the book, telling the stone cutter what to put on the slab. They are joined together at the hip, because neither can work without the other. And the ultimate end of that book is that suddenly the stonecutter realizes that he's made a mistake in the text. He's written the word "wing" in plural and he says "Oh Abu Said, I've ruined the text. I've ruined it. I'm so sorry." And Abu Said suddenly realizes his whole life has been about intellect. His whole life has been about rational thought—him being the extraordinary human being he was—and the text had been broken by the addition of this mistake. It's then that he realizes that in the story, the Book of Kingdoms, there was only one wing in the Book of Kingdoms that hovered above the opposing armies of the red, green, and yellow kingdoms—and even when I wrote that I didn't know why it was one wing, but it was going to be one wing, until I got to that point where he had made a mistake—and it was a plurality that was lacking in the first book—that finally came to realize itself in the second book. That pluralism is important to manifestation as much as the singular being in monolith of the wing. And so Abu Said just breaks down in laughter because he realizes he's fooled himself all his life believing in the unity of things, etc. etc. being a good Platonist that he was, but a stonecutter had got it right for him. That's sort of going back to that sense of stone as an embodiment of truth, which came out of a stone that he had to put an S on all the words that were in the text that he carved on the rock. So that's the metaphysic that was embedded in that text. People say oh well it's just an interesting device, but no. If you went back to the first book and realized—the first book with the Book of Kingdoms, they talked about the wing. Oh, yes, the wing, that's right. Well, now it's wings because you need double. You need all—balance, harmony—for metaphysical realism to work. It draws upon absurdity, but the irony of an intellectual giant like Abu Said in a cell where a stonecutter—he teaches him. I thought that's the irony of it. That the simple man often who seems to be on the surface a no-gooder, has much to teach the great intellect like my Aborigines taught me—they couldn't read or write. Couldn't head up. Didn't understand money. Give them $20, $100, they wouldn't know the difference. It's just yellow or blue. That was the irony of dealing with people with money. They didn't know what it was. Didn't care, but it got them food. So it was very practical. And that is the dichotomy between conceptualizing things on paper and allowing the intuition to determine. So even though I didn't know why it had to be only one wing, I just trusted my intuition. Somehow that problem would be solved. Where? 100,000 words later. That's why it ended up three books because I knew that in the first book, I hadn't finished joining all the things together, and so I had to do the three books. There were two generations of men and young men as well, so there was an inheritance, but underneath it all was that I had sense of the knower and the watcher. Some people were knowers and some were watchers. And that is a key to what you were talking about.

AV: That's a very different way of approaching it because it doesn't divide in the same way. In other words, a watcher of an Aboriginal ceremony is still a participant. May not necessarily be a knower, but still there isn't a division between the two, whereas what I was alluding to is more of an opposition between the exoteric and the esoteric and what you're suggesting is that actually if one thinks about things in terms of developing culture, or of shared culture, this distinction between watchers and knowers, which is closer to what Pythagoras referred to—those were hearers and those who knew, it is a very Pythagorean idea—is actually a way of bringing together. So there isn't *necessarily* an opposition—that opposition to some extent developed—and it's an interesting thing about your Kingdoms trilogy that that opposition is actually there in the monotheisms oftentimes. That is to say, a kind of literalistic interpretation of Christianity or Islam is often directly opposed to an esoteric tradition like Sufism, so you have a kind of bitter opposition between what we can call literalistic Islam on the one hand and mystical Islam or Sufism on the other, which manifests itself in contemporary times with sometimes people going so far, from the literalistic side, as to blow up shrines of the Sufi saints because they're offensive somehow. It goes that far in the contemporary Islamic world, but what you're suggesting is by implication there is another way, even within monotheism itself, which your trilogy suggests and that is that the monotheisms themselves can be understood as having this dimension of knowers and watchers, but it isn't necessarily an opposition.

JC: No, I agree with that. It is true. I remember one of the characters in the first book is Gustaf Magnussen who's living in Rome and he meets John of Chester who's our copyist and major hero. He finds that this fellow Gustaf is trying to write down the history of trolls, jogowits, and elves in Sweden. Right? He's attached to the Vatican, but he's doing it as an objective behavior in order to help to make the bells ring in Sweden better, so if he can debunk the system of the Pagans, he would have done his job. But in reality, Magnus was so absorbed with this Pagan world, he was cloaking as a pretense under scholastic activity and he talks about the Isle of Thule in the book. And that how Thule has got two tribes on it, but each tribe is complementary to the other. One tends the fire and keeps things warm. Another one goes out to sea and sails, and these two somehow join together on an island called Cronium, which is the island of Thule—Cronium. But it was a very difficult chapter to write I might add—to get it right. I realized that if you just change one letter in that name, you had the Sea of Cranium—the sea of thought where this island was sitting. And Magnus realized that when he was called out by John of Chester and said—because he asked John of Chester to help him write it because he's a copyist. And John says I don't know about this. I think you're actually really involved with these elves and things and he calls him out. And Gustaf realizes he's been outed because he's gone back to an ancient metaphysic to save himself from his Catholic environment through projecting on to this ideal landscape, which is Thule. And so in a way, it was the language change that made me realize that I had it—I eventually got the chapter because I realized that "Cranium" and "Cronium" were wonderfully allusive words, and the reason I did that is because when I study the map of Thule, it looked like a cranium. It's not round. It actually looked like a human head and I thought my God, nobody knows this mystical place actually looks like somebody's head! It's like thought! So you can see how the intuition finally allows that proposition to enter literature. Takes a long time sometimes. You have to really work over because you have to get rid of the realism. You've got to get it exact. You've got to find the right metaphors to make it happen. I had a conversation between the characters to finally reveal it—it's not logical. It's purely metaphysical realism. That's the way we are and that's another example of the way I struggled particularly with *Snow on the Camino Real* to get the language. It was much easier to write those, because in a sense I'd worked the language out. I got the characters. I didn't have to go through the process and they became progressively more realistic, but at the same time, they were not. They ultimately ended in conversation on an upstairs veranda in Jerusalem between three young men, who were the sons, nephews, and wards of the three guys who were now dead from the first book. And they are having to resolve becoming watcher-knowers in their age, so that the future goes on. So I wanted that sense that there was a future for us all in becoming knowers—how to watch—and they all of them acknowledged that they were already halfway there. One was a farmer—the nephew of John of Chester was a farmer and he had never left England before in his life. In the end, he learns so much and realized that these landscapes back in England were a metaphysical landscape that he had been cultivating as a young man—the sheep, the fields, and things like that. So he took back from those dialogues on the roof of the house in Jerusalem, and the other young fellow Omar went back to Mecca and realized, "I'm going back to head my father's tariqa and make into a genuine esoteric environment again and renew it," so he learned from his discussion with the other fellows who were friends of his father's. So that was wonderful—the worlds that I was creating between characters from the past, characters in the present, they all interlocked in the end. Nobody was really outside of the world, if you'd like. This whorl that you alluded to with those churingas.

AV: The spiral.

JC: Yes, the spiral.

AV: The whorl. The interlocking connected—one could say whorls. One could say worlds. All interlocking and interconnected and it's striking that another word for "knower" of course is a Greek term, gnosis. And one could refer to what you were talking about as—

JC: Gnosial knowledge.

AV: That's right. The watchers' and the knowers' movement from you could say exoteric to esoteric, but also knowers meaning those who know, gnosis as knowledge of what is hidden. The hidden connection. That which transcends the connection between subject and object. It's beyond that, which is what's symbolized in these connected whorls. These spirals that are linked and the whole goes beyond each of the individual parts.

JC: That's correct and embedded in those books is a sword—a scimitar. That's straight out of medieval thinking—to embody a sword that had certain magical properties that could turn into a book and not be a book, and eventually in that book, becomes a sword of militarism, kills somebody on the way to Jerusalem when some pirates invade the ship and it becomes a sword. And so it was the Word in terms of the original Book of Kingdoms, which is in the first book, and it becomes a magical sword. It is embedded in the book in the pillow of the lovers before, on their first night and Abu Said to his young wife says I felt something hard under my pillow last night. And she said it was a book. It was the Book of Kingdoms, but she was conceiving the fact the sword was his gift to his uncle as part of the dowry, but it transforms itself into a book. So I was contemplating with all those magical realist aspects too, but it's entirely plausible in tune with the landscape I've already set up, that these two lovers could find a sword in the book, which are perfect metaphors, underneath a pillow on the wedding night. So I was playing with all those sorts of things and so ultimately, they are teased out in the third novel and become resolved in Jerusalem by the three young men who finally hand [things] back. One hands back the Book of Kingdoms to Omar because his father was the one that translated it out of Persian. And the sword is given by John of Chester back to Omar because his father had given him—but he also gave him back the original text because he says it's better for you to take it back to its origin in Palestine because he received it from a Muslim on the shores of Galilee—his grandfather during the Battle of Hattin. So I was always trying to find a way to get the Book back into the East again after its sojourn in the West and nobody could read it. It was always about the non-legible non-readable Book, which these fellows finally tease out, that holds six characters. That was the mystery. This Book, even though the Book appears in the first book and you can read it. Its symbolism is so powerful and potent that it takes two other books to get the resolutions that that Book embodied—all is one. I think it was classic line of the ancient texts—all is one, one is all, and multiplicity comes out of unity which is basically what the Book of Kingdoms itself was. So you can see what I'm playing with when I say that ultimately you are breaking down the relationship between objects, which in this case is a scabbard and a sword and a book. And allowing them to enter a space that is entirely metaphysical, that partakes on the surface in its realism, which is the sword and the book, but ultimately, they are like the spirit Hakekit. They go through the whole three texts and permeate everything that these characters get involved with. And once I found that language it was easy to do, because suddenly you're always in it. You're always writing from that perspective. And nothing is not fair game. There's a chapter in the third volume where they end up in a monastery in Greece where the three men find themselves presented with a hand of John Chrysostum in a silver reliquary, and a young Hakim, who is the poet in the third volume—he's born as a Moor, brought up as a Christian and educated as a Jew because of his relationship with John of Tudela. I wanted him to embody all three religions and therefore be free of everything, so he could be a poet whereas the others—there's a farmer from England. The other ones are emerging from Mecca. They're already locked into their tradition, which they acknowledge at the end. You are the only free one amongst us because you are a poet and you are being brought up by three different religious traditions and anyway, they go up into this monastery—and the hand is presented by an Orthodox monk. And he says to young Hakim, you can kiss it. You can all kiss it. And they all kiss it and Hakim is completely—not destroyed. But he's absolutely—his whole lips become fire and he can't understand he just kissed a piece of rotting flesh from the fourth century or fifth century.

And he knows something strange has happened. The others kiss it and yes that's great, but the monk immediately recognized something is happening. He says how do you feel? He said, well, I felt these strange things on my lips. And the monk just looks at him and said, in essence, you are the only one—you are a knower. He doesn't say that in the book, but I'm saying he recognizes, "you're a knower. You have touched spirit in this mutilated hand." Now that hand I encountered on Mount Athos in the 1960s in a monastery called Philotheou. It was brought out for me to kiss. And it had a profound effect upon me—this hand. I've carried that hand in my mind for forty-odd years. And I relocated it to a monastery in central Greece—just take it and put it somewhere else—that's what you do as a writer. You don't worry about the historical existence of the hand in Mount Athos, and that's the freedom that metaphysical realism gives you—just take the hand from me. It's a hand. It's got a legitimate purpose in Mount Athos. It's got a legitimate purpose in my book—that sense of freedom that our friend the young Hakim of Toledo is able to express and so that last book—finally he becomes the poet that he has to become. And so there are twenty-five of his poems in that book. He wrote—the end of the book is his whole compendium of poems, which explore this strange relationship between being born a Muslim, then Christian, and Jewish. His parents died. He was brought up by Christians who couldn't afford to keep him, so he ends up in the streets of Toledo where Benjamin of Tudela finds him and makes him his little servant and then he teaches him language because he couldn't read or write. And I was fascinated with that sense that out of nothing, a great poet could be born. Does that make sense to you? The transformative effect of being free of the constraint of culture if you'd like. Hakim of Toledo embodies that as a young man and as poet in the book. I wanted a poet to be there somehow, but the hand is part of that metaphysical realism that I was talking about earlier. So all of those books are full of metaphysical realism, but it's so much more layered now that you think it's actually real.

AV: Ultimately, it's also about freedom and about being free and perhaps that's a good place to draw this part of the conversation to a close.

JC: Yes, that's a good thought—that finally the difficult thing is to become free, personally and creatively.

Third Conversation:

TIMELESSNESS

JC: Yesterday we finished on the theme of freedom, didn't we? And that was the end of a fairly remarkable conversation about metaphysical realism, but we wanted to go further than that. We wanted to explore, as I suggested, that theory of lights. You have read those Sufi texts about the mysticism of light. What was your reaction to those Sufi texts?

AV: The text focused on Muhammad as not a historical, but a revelatory figure, and referred to pre-existence—existence prior to existence. And to illumination—different aspects of illumination of light. One aspect of it is that it represents a dimension within Islam that, even though it's in Islamic language, is referring to the light, which is not specifically a Muslim category alone. So there is kind of a paradoxical dimension to it. On the one hand, it's a passage that's clearly in a Muslim context and at the same time, it's a passage about what you could call philosophy of light or religion of light. I would actually, of the two, prefer the term religion of light because philosophy today more or less exclusively implies analytical thought and this is visionary.

JC: And that's interesting. The elements within it were quite fascinating in that while he was talking about the lights in plural, I think actually this is the first place I've come across the sense of lights rather than the light, which is very much a monotheistic vision of light. This sense of duplication of light struck me as very interesting because it seemed to me, he was touching on almost a kind of spiritualized materialism in the sense that the light he was talking about was not the light of the visible light that we know, but rather acknowledges what they call specks of dust. I think that's the expression that was used.

AV: Particles.

JC: Yes, that's right and that struck me as a kind of crossover between the physical, or if you'd like, the organic and the spiritual. And he talks about prime matter too in the sense that from light issue all existent things, and it says here God created the light of Muhammad from his light. He formed it and brought it forth at his own hand. This light remained before God for 100,000 years, during which time, he beheld it, 70,000 glimpses and glances every day and night, and with each glance he formed it into a new light and created from there all existent beings. So in fact this light that we're talking about actually does have the capacity to make nature. It's not just a spiritual light *per se*. It's more than a spiritual light. Did you get that sense too?

AV: It's embedded. It's the substrate or the basis for nature, which emerges from light.

JC: Yes, now that to me is really quite revolutionary, even though it's very old as a thought. To me, now, this sense that light—I don't know a lot about astrophysics or indeed astroscience, but my sense is that the science itself is beginning to recognize more subtlety associated with light in its physical realm too. Have you got that sense that there's beginning to be a reversion or a crossover back to that ancient concept that we engage with here?

AV: It's possible, but one of the things that occurs to me when looking at something like that from within Sufism is that there is another tradition, which is directly connected with light and sees light as absolutely central and that is Manichaeism. And Manichaeism is actually described as a religion of light. So, there's a sense in which when you're talking about religion of light—or philosophy of light, if you want—it's something that transcends any particular tradition. It's a different kind of science. I think contemporary scientific exploration still ultimately is grappling with a world of cause and effect and of—ultimately applications in the material world. Some aspects of quantum theory—quantum mechanics—tie in with that, but it's still quantum mechanics. And I think what we're talking about, which is metaphysics in the sense of *ta meta ta phusika*, the transcendence of the physical, means that although scientific exploration starts to move in that direction inevitably, it can only reach so far and then beyond that, it requires visionary experience you can call it. So there are two realms that are meeting, but the one doesn't penetrate very far into the other in the same way that, for the most part, Manichaeism or Sufism—you don't have coming out of that any mechanics.

JC: Yes, I see what you're saying. So it remains still in that esoteric environment rather than breaking out into the conscious world—

AV: As something pragmatic, for the most part. Although there are miraculous dimensions.

JC: That's suggested too, I suppose. But it is important to me that sense of lights be a palpable reality within this domain of the spirit rather than just be a palpable reality. This is what it seems to me that these philosophers are getting at—these Moorish philosophers. That they recognize the light they talk about has a pre-existence. They do talk about pre-existence. I find that very interesting—the idea that there is a Muhammad before existence. I don't think that in the Christian tradition, we talk about a Christ before Christ. He's still firmly embedded in history even though—in a way, he's in less history than Muhammad because we know much more about Muhammad in terms of his daily life, etc. That pre-existence of Christ is not emphasized in Christianity, but here it was, so I thought that was quite an exciting idea that the primordial essence is already formed or fashioned prior to existence and manifests itself in lights.

AV: Yes, I think that part of what you're referring to is the division between—on the one hand, literalist Christianity where the notion of a Christ before existence would be completely alien and then different variants of mystical Christianity where that does exist—or at least can exist, the same in Islam actually. There are more literalistic forms of Islam and more extreme versions, like fanatical Salafism or Wahhabism, and then there is esoteric Islam like the Sufism you're talking about. But there's something that ties in with that and that is Platonism because the Platonic tradition, including Neoplatonism, is what informs and is behind a passage like you're talking about. It's not always widely recognized because it's not necessarily convenient for a particular religious tradition—traditions tend to be reluctant to acknowledge that some of what they're drawing from is actually from outside the tradition, but there's something really remarkable about Platonism and particularly Neoplatonism in terms of what it makes possible, and what it fertilizes, so I think that kind of religious philosophy of light—there referring to origin of light—is at least inflected by a Neoplatonic philosophical tradition that's quite extraordinary really. And again, all of these are by and large, excluded from much discussion these days. In other words, by beginning with that passage and then going in this direction, our conversation is moving into areas that for most people—even if they're adherents of Islam for example—would be almost completely unknown. So what is it that you see as connecting religion of light, or that kind of illumination passage, to literature?

JC: Yes, that's interesting. Clearly my own experience is that there is a pathway towards the imaginal reality that you can capture as a writer in the imaginative sense—that's associated with these lights. That is, to me, quite important because up to a point, I would have never considered the idea that pure metaphysics could have a place in literature. I can understand it being alluded to like in *Brothers Karamazov*, or some of the great books by Dostoevsky and others by modern writers like Huysmans who suggested things in his later books, like *La Cathédrale*. But it's never metaphysics as metaphysics clothed in fictive garb. It's more like a statement of didacticism in the text and that's what I would think is very important—that this kind of thought process alludes to—is that you're not necessarily talking about light as a metaphor in this text, which is often what it is in other dispensations. You're talking about light having both an impalpable and palpable reality outside of any suggested symbol. And that is the quality that I think literature has yet to embrace—how to get into that—how to access that beautiful theory that lies in theology, if you'd like, and make it into a fictive reality. So my sense that we've still got a long way to go to get that condition operating outside of allegory—the conventional allegory or conventional symbolism within a book that can be easily alluded to. It's something else, that quality and that elseness, so to speak, is this light. And whether it means that the writer—and this is taking it one step further—has to be in himself or herself vatic, and acknowledge that they are inhabited by vates, and that their sense of seeing and acknowledging that as needing—not necessarily a tool in the conscious sense or in the advantageous sense, because once you go to that area, you're already taking advantage of things. I'll take some LSD to do this or do that. That's completely against any spiritual reality. It's just a physiological excitement to go into those things. My sense is that the writer has to own up to the need to be deeply spiritual in his engagement with what he's doing. Now that's very hard for a modern writer. Very hard, as you know, for most writers. They can either confess an easy-going Catholicism or Protestantism and say yes, well I do believe and I go to church. That's the exoteric side of their character, but we're not talking about that when we're talking the writer as vates. He has to access a different level of spirituality and make it work on the page, and that I think is the challenge for the future of writing. So that's why the passage on light struck me as valuable, I suppose. That's why I immediately went to reading it because I thought, well, there's something about the specks of light like dust on the ground. Seemed to me a very palpable reality that we had not engaged in in the past and wanted to get your thoughts on it too because you've got a broader experience of Buddhism than I have. You might have seen echoes of that, particularly in terms of esoterism within the European context, you might've seen things that alluded to that as well.

AV: There are, actually. And one of the things I would mention consequent on what you were referring to is that I'm not quite so quick to dismiss psychedelics. Not because I'm using psychedelics or drawing on them myself, but because that too is an area where in the contemporary world, there was this kind of flowering in the 1960s of experimentation and then a tremendous suppression, and so for thirty or forty years, possession of a mushroom, which grows naturally in the environment, became a class one felony in the United States, for example, and so too in Great Britain and elsewhere. And so you have a history of the use of mushrooms, which are directly connected to the themes that we are talking about. Traditionally, there are aspects which are unique to, for example, Mexico, but then there's also speculation about the use of them in the UK where they grow naturally, a variant of psilocybin. I mention this because our collective assumptions are shaped by this kind of extended historical suppression. I'm not convinced—I had been convinced at one time that this is a simply a side road and it's not something to explore really at all. At this point, for a whole variety of reasons, I've changed my perspective on that. I'm more open to the idea that for some people, it may be the case that something like psilocybin or some other, preferably naturally, but perhaps not, occurring substance may be an avenue into the kind of thing that we're talking about. Or accentuate or provide a dimension of something which otherwise that individual may not have access to. So I say that because this theme of illumination and lights is part of the phenomenon. It's an aspect of the phenomenon associated with, especially, psilocybin mushrooms, but more broadly, also with some other psychedelics. And here, I am not suggesting that they're all the same. There is a vatic dimension to that. There's a professor of religious studies that's a bit of an outlaw named Chris Bache, who has done twenty years of experimentation in this area, and his work can be described as vatic. Now, all of that said, my own approach is very much more in terms of meditation and practices from the realm specifically of Vajrayana and more broadly Buddhism. And there also, you do have traditions concerning light and lights—illumination. And again, in both cases, what we're talking about are experiential dimensions. In other words, psychedelics are experiential. Seeing the lights—having experience of light, having experience of vastness, and being released from individual identity—same is true within Buddhism in that there are practices just like in hesychastic tradition in Orthodoxy that include phenomena concerning lights and also illumination. And one of those has to do also with light surrounding us, so for instance, the image of that is the halo. It's angelic illumination: the manifestation of non-physical beings, angels, are illuminatory. There are experiences of spiritual light—those who are praying, there are stories about monks in the hesychastic tradition who almost blind someone approaching them, so there are experiential dimensions that manifest in the physical world and all of that ties in I think with what you're referring to as vatic, which breaks the purely intellectualized dimension of our subject. And I think what you're suggesting is that all of these things are experiential, are in the purview of the writer, and need to be in literature. That is, literature is not an area of diversion that exists on its own separate from all of these things. It has these things within its purview.

JC: Yes, and that was perfectly expressed, that literature has to actually extend itself beyond its literary existence. That's why I find Victor Segalen so important because he's acknowledging that vatic element of his work, as a doctor, as an explorer, and also as a writer. And while he would never use the word "vatic," it's clear that he was conscious of having to break with the old forms that were around him at the time. Even though I don't think he was fully aware of that, as a conscious literary activity, I think it was more to do with his need to give expression to this extreme sense of the lights, if you'd like, that he wanted to make into a palpable reality in literature. And not many writers have done that. Not many writers in the last hundred years in fact. We have tried to go to that place because they either say it is being debilitating in the sense of secularism and secularism needs to maintain its earthbound push towards the future and writers in general might acknowledge and accept that they have a religious background, but they would never say that religious background per se is forcefully entering their work. Not in a didactic or theological or a dogmatic level, but rather the force of it in their spirit should be in the text, but they won't go there yet, because they are still hesitant about the declaration of spirit in work. And I've encountered that myself because in the public domain when you talk about these things, people are a bit sort of taken aback, but you are such an intellectual and write in such a way and you write about all these other things. I said "Yes, but everything in those books has always been pushed by this impetus towards the vatic and towards the spirit." And they say. "Oh, right. Okay, but it's not religious?" I say it's not—it is religious, but it's not religious. It's beyond that easy tag that you put on it with the word "religion." It's going beyond that and that's where literature I think has an important role to play now in declaring itself once again as a vatic activity rather than just a literary activity.

AV: One of the things that strikes me about that is the word "religion," and I'm a little reluctant—even in referring to *Religion of Light*, which is a title of a book I wrote—I'm still reluctant in many respects to use that term for what we're talking about. You've used the terms "metaphysical realism" and "metaphysical"—and also referred us to the subject of light or the theme of light that transcends particular traditions. The word "religion" really, the way it's used today, refers mostly to socio-cultural manifestations, to beliefs, to particular doctrines and so on. And that's not what we're talking about. We're talking about the vatic in the sense of referring to the realm that transcends or nearly transcends the realm of language itself. But that you're expressing through language. And that's what's happening in that passage you referred to. He's capturing or seeking to allude to in language this realm in which Muhammad pre-exists Muhammad. And I think what you're suggesting is that Victor Segalen in some respects, some—by his linguistic experiments and by his relentless exploration and then transformation of that—was doing something not exactly the same but similar. Similar. Can you elaborate on that because you've seen Segalen as so important in your own experience?

JC: I think that this goes back further than Segalen, because he goes back to a time when I felt as a writer, you wrote in a dimension which was entirely literary, and that you were conscious of that activity, so therefore it fell into line with all of the rules and regulations that determined the literary process. But when I came into contact with Aborigines, I felt that I was living most of the time in the gap between literature and life and that I was constantly orchestrating the two in order to find some resolution. But Aborigines and tribal peoples—they don't live in the gap. Their life and their life experiences are wedded to the Dreaming and so they don't have any consciousness of being in this gap and then referring to the Dreaming on one level and life at another level; rather, they fully integrate the two. Whereas that division is the normal process of [our] rational thought. We live a religious life or we live a spiritual life—but we live a physical life as well and we try to juggle them.

AV: And they're somehow separated.

JC: They're always separated and then the thing I learned from travel is that in an indigenous perspective, there's no separation. Modern psychologists say well, that's because they don't have all the accoutrements of psychiatry and psychology and the self-referentiality that we have since Descartes, etc. All very good. I can accept that at a certain logical level, but at another level, I realize that the imposition of the Dreaming and the acceptance of the Dreaming—it squeezed out any sense that you needed to conduct a dialogue between the two. That to me was profoundly moving because I realized that as a writer, I was not doing that. I was living on the surface of literature. I was not risking all as an Aborigine might do when he plunges into the Dream every time he does a dance to so to speak—to get it right. It's burning me. The physicality of being physically burned during a Dreaming ceremony strikes me as a very fascinating crossover but they wouldn't allow that not to happen. They wanted to be burned as they became spiritualized in the Dreaming. So Segalen comes on much later in that sense, because I'd already been where Segalen was, but he articulated it in his particular fashion, and I realized that he was trying to get rid of that space between the language and the reality that he was trying to express. He wanted to close that gap and that to me—few writers have done in my estimation. They live very well in the literary domain—even a modern poet like Eliot or Ginsberg or somebody like that. They still live within that area where it's when you read the so-called translations of Chinese work by Segalen you realize it's his mind operating at this level of compactness between the reality he lives—the need to express our certain kind of metaphysic and the way to do it and then not even be conscious of the activity of doing it. That's the vatic aspect of the process of writing. And that's what I've realized is so important for the future of literature.

AV: There is another writer who comes to mind who also had that dimension. and that's Ezra Pound. Pound is someone who naturally and consciously drew together as much as he could of classical tradition: Greco-Roman tradition. He also drew on Chinese tradition, as Segalen did.

JC: Yes. Fascinating isn't it? They all did.

AV: Yes, in some respects—

JC: Saint-John Perse did.

AV: He did, but there's something distinctive about Pound, I think, and about what Pound's ambition was—what his aim was. Segalen and Pound do have that in common, and Saint-John Perse also, but Pound—I wondered if you could say something about Pound and how he figures in this idea of literature—going beyond the gap of literature as existing on more than just the page. Because Pound really did, as you say, risk all—and he was a vatic figure. There's no question about that. It's why he ultimately, for some period, was even confined to an asylum forcibly. He wasn't mad. It was a punishment. What would you have to say about Pound and his *Cantos* in relation to these themes and his being a vatic writer?

JC: It's interesting that you're bringing up Pound, Arthur, because he had deep influences on me ever since my late twenties when I first encountered him. I felt that Pound—you're right about the fact that Pound tried to break with all the old traditions and he did in a very strident way. There was no doubt that he had kind of megaphone voice with regard to some interests and obsessions, which sometimes get in the way of reason. But I was deeply impressed with his encounter with the Occitan people and the poems of the troubadours, or those great poems that he wrote before the *Cantos*. That struck me as very important because what he conveyed there, which is unique in fact to modern poetry, that I am here. I am in twelfth-century France. I am on the backstreet between here and the next town. And you, the reader, are with him. Absolutely on the road in Occitan. He closed the gap there between experience, as you referred to, and the literary effect that he was trying to attain, but he just closed it and he said it's no longer just about the word on the page, it's me—I'm the road—and he was the first. Eliot didn't do that. Eliot came from an Olympian viewpoint and any of the great poets—even Whitman—the great American—

AV: Walt Whitman.

JC: Whitman celebrates these things, but you never ultimately feel that he's there in it. It's just that he has a very good way of conveying the fact that he might be in it. Different thought. So I see that Pound is certainly the first American, but I think first in English language that actually exploited this sense of being there. So when he attached himself to anything in his work, particularly in the *Cantos*, whether it's economic theory, whether it's in essence history, whether it's the great medieval thinkers, you always feel that I am there. I am with you today John Scotus and we are discussing Platonism. And that again he closed the gap. And I really took that on board. I think that that—the *Cantos*—I don't understand the *Cantos*, probably 80% of it. Because its range of references are too great and I'm not prepared to go there to study.

I've got books on all the bits and pieces in there, but in the end, you're becoming an encyclopedist when you do that, but when he breaks through with his lyric, it's actually more complete and complex than anything that Homer did. People don't see that extraordinary mind and extraordinary eyesight and extraordinary sensibility that he must've developed. He wasn't born with it. That's another thing about the vatic activity. It's not naturally something that you're just born with. You have to refine every sensibility you've got to the point where your metaphors, your expressions are in themselves self-transcending. Homer did it too, but Homer did it in a different sort of way. Homer did it in a sort of vast celebration of life through the physicality—the glory of the physical, which is as profound in many ways as what we're talking about. But Pound did it at a level where you could feel a kind of emanation of spirit coming through the simple beautiful images he put on paper that far transcends all the political material that he threw in. I don't mind him going there through that stuff because I understand why he's doing it. He's trying to cut to the bottom of the vortex. You just can't come out with the illusion of beauty pulled on down by vanity—I say pull down—what a wonderful line—so full of trenchancy. He's taking it from somewhere else, but it doesn't matter. He made it his own because he closed the gap and in that sense, I think he's really the greatest twentieth-century poet, but not necessarily the most important. I make a slight distinction there that you can be truly great, but not necessarily the most important because most people weren't reading him.

It's incomprehensible, but people who love poetry, they know what he's trying to do and the experiment he's trying to do at every level, but it's vatic, definitely.

AV: There are people who also do what you're referring to—not necessarily in poetry or even in fiction. I'm thinking here of Ralph Emerson and Thoreau in particular and to some extent Bronson Alcott—I think the three of them—because the three of them are the founders of the American Renaissance—American Transcendentalism, which has a Platonic background. It emerged out of Platonism as much as, really more than, anything else. Asian religious traditions again played a role. For example, they were drawing to some degree more or less from Hinduism as it was emerging, but it was really the Platonic translations of Thomas Taylor more than anything else that inspired and drove what became known as Transcendentalism and there too, there's clearly what you're referring to as a vatic dimension. It's largely in a kind of hybrid prose that's not really conventional.

JC: It's experimental.

AV: It's experimental. Emerson's essays—and his poems—from the beginning to the very end of his life, they are forays. They're explorations. People don't realize that. By writing—he's also exploring—and there's a fusion. Emerson provides advice in his explorations of themes like *Society and Solitude*.

JC: *Nature*. What an extraordinary little book. Wonderful.

AV: It's wonderful. It is. And it's also an exploration into new territory when Thoreau goes to Walden. It's an exploration into new territory and it's on the one hand literature, on the other spiritual exploration fused.

JC: Accidentally, because in the end it's about the experience rather than I'm going to write a book about—

AV: That's right. It's about the experiential. Yes. And there isn't a gap between life and literature in *Walden.*

JC: No, I agree with that. I do agree with that because I can see now that there's an immediacy there and even though it's got its slight stylized fact—for instance, we also know that he didn't live there all the time. He made it appear that he lived there all the time, but that's how I'm walking down the street in the road to Parigor: Pound's in the twelfth century, but he's closed the gap and that sense of actually—what I referred to earlier in one of our conversations-—that by removing time from the sentence, you close the gap. And that's the hardest thing for a writer to do is to get rid of linearity in line and in sentence and in paragraph to the extent that you allude to time because it's always there, but it's actually being removed from the textual ease of the mind accepting the things on the page. And that's often when people say when you use those strange words, you constantly lace your text with Greek and Latin and I say I don't do that for a kind pseudo-effect of learning. I'm not interested in that. I'm only interested in the word—having within it such an explosive potential that you, the reader, have to be stopped in your tracks. Even if there are quotation marks around it. I'll always explain what the word means in the fluidity of the sentence, but the idea that you can remove time from language or from prose is to me what these guys are talking about in a certain kind of way. They're breaking with the habits of thoughts. And you're suggesting in the case of Emerson and Thoreau that they're doing a similar thing, not necessarily with time, but they are inadvertently doing it with time, particularly with Thoreau, because he walks out, goes home, has a shower, probably spends a week outside, then he goes back to the forest, but I don't care that he did that. He got it when he wrote it because he closed the gap, again. And that's fine with me. I don't think that a writer has to be as—what's the word? Calculated in his obsession with living every physical aspect of his experience.

AV: But the result is timeless—

JC: Yes.

AV: —in the sense that *Walden* or Emerson's essay is, whether they're popular or not popular. Currently they're in a period of being unpopular in the academic world. Not necessarily in the world of people who read for meaning and for joy. But the writings themselves are timeless in the sense that I think one can understand them as very much what you're referring to, which is time itself—they exist in a world of time, but there's also an aspect of existing in timelessness that infuses those works. That's what gives them their power. On the one hand, they are in time. And on the other hand, they're timeless not in a clichéd sense, but in a real sense.

JC: Time has in a sense been subsumed, by the timeless—and both of those ingredients—are not even concepts, they actually go beyond conception. It's we who conceive of them, because the Aborigine doesn't think about time. He has a limited capacity to add up. On one hand he can say—one, two, many things, but he doesn't actually say one, two, three, four, five, and then counts to fifty or we're going to have a month holiday or something. They have no sense of time and that really struck me that they could function outside of time. And I always remember when the old man would come to tell me a story of his painting. He'd put up beside me, he'd close the door, and then he'd say well this is my Dreaming, and we would enter a timeless space. Totally. And I'd be writing it down on the computer or by hand and I'd always remember thinking as I was doing that, do you realize where you are? Right at this moment? Take and savor it. Because time does not exist in the mind of this man as he speaks and tells you the story of an aspect of time, which is the creation of that landscape. So it's not even a disjoint in the end. It's a complete erosion of the idea of time and eternity and that's the quality that seems to me that language can and should be able to embrace eventually. Not necessarily in my time, but what I am getting at is we're all experimenting in the realm of the physical and the intellectual against the challenge that we've set ourselves, and I think that people like the people we've talked about—Thoreau and Emerson and a few other writers of their time, Thomas Taylor, enormously important man that people never even talk about, but the work he did was exceptional—they lived in this vatic area. They constantly challenged themselves.

AV: So on the one hand, we've been talking about fiction and how fiction can be a manifestation of what we're referring to here as the vatic, but in the case of Emerson and Thoreau, it's in an area that you can call non-fiction, but non-fiction doesn't really describe it. Non-fiction is a sort of flat term that doesn't really indicate the kind of mysterious—

JC: It's a crossover now.

AV: Sometimes people use the term creative non-fiction, but there really isn't a category for this realm of letters—

JC: That we're talking about.

AV:—that we're talking about. But it's not journalism obviously. It's not just reporting and it's not fiction, yet it's also got this creative dimension and simultaneously in the case of Emerson, it's the exploration of ideas and of the life of action combined with contemplation. It's a very distinctive kind of approach in a different way. I wondered what you had to say about that in terms of your own work. Do you see where I'm driving?

JC: Yes, I do. I know where you're driving, and I think the aspect of fiction that is entirely different to the writing of prose—is that fiction carries within it a savor, a taste that lingers long after the text has been written or put down. Prose doesn't. In reading Batchelor, I said well, the more I read Batchelor, the less I like it.

AV: Stephen Batchelor.

JC: Stephen Batchelor, yes. The less I like it because I know he's merely taking me into a prosy environment that's informed of course by his wonderful knowledge of Buddhism, etc., but it's not allowing ellipsis to take hold of my being. Fiction does. Genuine literary fiction. You walk away from it feeling an entirely different person, even if a minute, or ten minutes, or a year, or sometimes thirty or forty years. Some books never go away from you. You can't say that about any other form of prose, but you know that something has been retained like a piece of knowledge—a pebble in an old street in Florence. You know it's there and you feel it as you walk down the street. It's indefinable. That's what this kind of fiction and poetry needs to—it does—express, and in essence Pound and the writers we're speaking of do that because they are entirely removed from a sensibility that requires it to remain here with us here on this world. That's—I think that's an acquired sensibility. I also believe that writers don't realize sometimes that they actually have to do a lot of work to refine their sensibility. They think, well, I know I'm not a reader—but I can pick up techniques and I can put together a plot, etc. I say, "Yes but what have you done about your sensibility?" They say, "What do you mean?" I mean it's actually another word to be used in terms of a technique of work and language. I say well, sensibility allows you to close that gap that we're talking about in your mind so that intuition comes in and slowly but surely refines the techniques that you've already got and acquired to a point when you are like the point of the pencil on the page. You are so sharp in terms of what you're going to do that your sensibility has taken you to that point, but it takes many, many, many years to acquire sensibility and it's indefinable how you acquire it except that you must be conscious that you need to acquire it. There are steps in this process so when you're in a foreign environment, you're sitting at a table in a cafe or you're sitting at a rock in the desert or wherever, you suddenly put your mind to work on your sensibility. Not as an act of revery; that's different altogether. It's the way that particular space is embracing you and how you're receiving it and what you're doing with it in terms of language. That's the process of developing a conscious sensibility that you will then later apply to work, so that's why we travel. It's not because it's different. As Segalen says, it's not interesting to be different or the difference. And in fact, it's boring quite often. But you're constantly placing your nerve endings, your spiritual nerve endings, if you'd like, on notice about the world around in order to translate that world around into something that's wholly refined in terms of sensibility for it.

AV: And that can happen also in this kind of experimental fiction which Thoreau wrote—it's experimental non-fiction rather. That's what Thoreau was doing to some extent, but Thoreau did it by going to Walden.

JC: And *Week on the Concord and Merrimack River* too, didn't he?

AV: That's right. And Segalen did on the other hand did it by going to China and riding across China 1000 miles or something like that. And I—

JC: 1,500 miles.

AV: Something like that. It is extraordinary. And it leads me to the question what is the role of travel and exploration and encountering the other or the exotic as Segalen was referring to it—what's the role of that in terms of refining sensibility? How is it that travel and exploration tie into sensibility?

JC: I think they are absolutely seamless really. That's why the great travelers are often some of the best writers. You've heard of people like Richard Burton who in himself was a great traveler and Speke, and people that went up the Nile. These people could write well too in the domain where they were, but you could see that the world they went into had a profound effect upon them and the travel in a sense is a capacity to remove yourself from the normal constraints of your life. You're not living in a fantasy world. You're living in a world that's other than the life that you normally lead. And that is the nature of the voyage. Segalen wrote a book called *In the Land of the Real* which is not an exact translation, but as an English word, "real" is actually an interesting one. The Land of the Real, capital R, is that world but it's also the world that it appears, that's what he's really writing about, both of them. He's not terribly interested in temples and things like that. He's really interested in what those things represent. My sense is that travel in my own life has been enormously important as a vehicle not only for discovering places, but for writing places. Most of my journals are full of the meditations I'm having as I'm on the move. Now in the early years, those books were full of what I saw, how I saw. Well, fine, that was a part of translating and determining sensibility because you start to use your eyes, your ears more actively. I don't carry cameras. And you use your hand as your artifice, but as the years rolled on, the work became more and more inward in the travel. There are references to where I am, etc. But quite often necessarily, I mention Luxor, the 22nd of May, or something like that and I'm walking to a temple, but what that temple is telling me, for example was about words on pillars. I finally realized that the architecture is now being determined by language. It's not just a pretty picture of nice things, it's whole classic beautiful words on stone that are going back to your megalithic environment. So travel allows you to absolutely go beyond the boundaries of the norm and go beyond the boundaries of the acceptable. You can try and actually press your mind into doing sort of strange gymnastics in a journal when you're traveling.

It's not just a record of events and places and spaces. Quite often when I do a very serious journey, I've written copious notes. When I come back and do the book, I hardly go to the notes. It's almost as though the notes have embedded everything so solidly in my mind, I don't really have to read the notes. It's funny, but if I just pass through that and camera'd it, I wouldn't have that sense of closing this—the gap—again. So traveling—your diary and your pen are a part of that acquiring of no gap at all, so to speak, and I think it's enormously important.

AV: And it's also breaking of the routine, of the ordinary, of the familiar and that's what Segalen was doing because by going to China in those days, he was compelling himself to break free. And there's an element of freedom from as well as freedom to. Those are intertwined.

JC: I agree with that. Very interesting thought. Each person has what Kathleen Raine used to say is a kind of imaginal topography, in that we carry a landscape within us, which is our particular obsession as writers or indeed thinkers probably—but certainly as poets. And that may be China or it may be Morocco—in my lifetime, there have been certain places, but then slowly as I grew more mature, the places merged into one and so I didn't need to go to anywhere in particular to feel that that was going to give me the sort of experiences both internally and in métier as a writer. I didn't need to worry any more because you're just floating on a surface. Your meditations are on paper in this world, but also in the metaphysical world, even if you were in a dirty hotel in Luxor or wherever—there are two worlds that you live in and quite often a dirty hotel yields the best writing. Get a modern hotel and you completely—you've conflated it upon yourself as soon as you walk in the room, and so I've always had a principle of tending to live in very simple circumstance when I'm traveling, and that has helped. That sharpens your senses.

AV: There's a term that was coined by Henry Corbin and those who conveyed his work, which comes out of the tradition with which we started, that is to say Persian and later Moorish and North African Sufism. And it has to do, not with the imagination, but with the imaginal as this point of juncture between transcendence and immanence. The imaginal is not simply fantasy. It's not revelatory alone. It's also an actual faculty of perception and a point of juncture between realms, that exists as an interworld. "Interworld" sometimes translates the term *barzakh*, and there are poets who I think also have entered into that kind of imaginal space with or in their poetry, and one of course is Rilke in the *Sonnets to Orpheus* and *Duino Elegies*, extraordinary poems. There is a sense in which that poetry is imbued with encounter with the other—not in the sense of what is separate from us, but in the sense of direct revelation. Those are revelatory works that were revealed to Rilke. They are in some ways the summation of his life's work. And this term "imaginal" is valuable because it provides us with a kind of term for the spiritual topography that you're referring to and you've explored in your Kingdoms trilogy and then also in a book called *Palace of*

Memory. You've explored the imaginal in different ways, which again is not separated from this—what we began with, which is the theme of spiritual light. It's not separated from it, nor is the term "imaginal" separated from it. In fact, Corbin by that term expressed something very much along these exact lines of illumination, experience of different lights in this interworld in between the physical and the transcendent and I wondered how that term imaginal in the kind of terrain we're talking about—this kind of spiritual topography as it were—manifests in these particular forms of fiction.

JC: It very much does and I think it's a very good point that you made that the trilogy in particular—but also *Palace*—the landscape that's in those books is very large. It spreads from Chester to Mecca—from Luxor to Córdoba, from Rome to Sweden and Ultima Thule—the whole of Europe and the Mediterranean are in the three books. In other words, I wanted the whole world metaphorically to be compressed into these books, not only through the fact that these three men represented Judaism, Christianity, and Islam as the three protagonists. They therefore expanded into this whole world and they brought this whole known world into that inn. There is that wonderful term of the Jewish Kabbala, *tsim tsum*. They talk about contraction. That's a particular word for divine contraction. It reflects the idea that when God manifests himself to human beings, he contracted himself to create the world so that they could be close together. Beautiful idea. We normally talk about the reverse—but Jews had this other sense of it and my feeling was that I could bring the world into sight through the intellects of these extraordinary different men—full of personalities, individuals with whom you can identify very strongly. All of them experienced a disappointment in love. All of them transcend that disappointment in different ways—these three men. I wanted that aspect to be a part of these books too, but the world had to be put into the books and that was the big challenge to make that possible. That's the realism, so-called, behind metaphysical realism. That you are capable of putting the whole world into one place into a remote inn, during a period of sixty to seventy hours, because it was time-centered too in that sense—that they were only there for long weekends so to speak with the snow around them, and then the snow suddenly melted and they were free to go. So the contraction of the weather had brought them into this little inn run by the Jew, Benjamin, who was an ever-giving man and the others manifested their humanity in different ways, one through the intellect in Abu Said, and the other one through his dogged perseverance, John of Chester. So I wanted to break with that sense that a writer could only position his novel in London in 1946 or whatever—for instance, in a small village in France and say no, no. The whole world should be in a book. Not just one small segment that you've chosen. So that was the background as to why there is such an expansive mode in those three books and the use of texts is visible in the Book of Kingdoms, but you've got to remember that Abu Said was deeply influenced by his mentor Ibn Tufail, who had written that wonderful book about the young boy that grew up and had no language at all, but was able to get all of philosophy through experiential knowledge, so each one had some kind of armrest that they leant on in terms of texts. In the case of Benjamin of Tudela, he was wondering around the world acquiring the names of all the Jews that he had met because he wanted to make a text, but he was deeply influenced by Ibn Gabirol, who was his inspiration because he was going to go out to find the bones of Ibn Gabirol, which were buried under a fig tree, but he could never find them. So again, intellectual things have to be important for a book—and each character bears his own philosophy if you like, but he's also bearing his mentors because they are important to what a character is—just as to who we are. I acknowledge—you acknowledge your great mentors throughout life. Why shouldn't they be in a book too? So that's why these characters all have a prop upon which they lean.

AV: It's also, though, that there's also a kind of camaraderie beyond time, whereas that it's common for us today to think about—if we think about Plato at all, or Homer, as someone who existed very long ago and is a kind of author of a frozen text, and we don't think of them as, in some sense, alive or present or as comrades or friends and the same would be true of Plotinus or of many others. But I think that's an illusion in some sense or it's a projection. The reality is that as we become familiar and then become close to these writers of the past, we experience them in a different way, so it's not only that these are mentors that you're referring to, it's that there's a kind of shared communion of the spirit we could say and that's—

JC: You've closed the gap.

AV: It's irrespective of particular social or geographic or religious divisions. That's part of what's happening in your books.

JC: And achieved this combination really in *Palace of Memory*, where I envisage the construction—the re-construction—of a paradise garden in the mind of the narrator, who is referring back to the twelfth century to a god that was created by a king—he as a god of man, so he had this double identity. I was fascinated with the doppelgänger in that sense. But another man who's between them, who is trying to revive the garden, who slowly but surely found himself absorbed into the garden, right? And then ultimately to express the garden in the book so that suddenly a Virgil and Dante motif comes into play where Roberto the narrator finds at his shoulder is Don Francesco, whose work he's been studying in order to understand the garden constructed by the King. So they're walking through the garden together, and Don Francesco starts to introduce him—there's Ibn Gabirol and a tortoise shell over here, and everybody nods to one another, and so that gap that we talk about—the historicist character of mind—has been eliminated by this surreal adventure in the garden, because I wanted to say that these people actually are my friends. I quite often say to people, "Well, I've had a time talking to Plato today," and they think you're a nut, but you're not, because you're saying they exist for me right now and they are alive to me right now. They are not in the fifth century B.C. at all. That's the thing: it takes a long time to reach that point though. You acknowledge how difficult it is to find a way through to allow—to extrude—what is the word? To get rid of time between you and he and she.

AV: So really the theme that ties much of what we've been talking about together is the theme of time and transcendence of time. Time and timelessness. More even in some ways, referring to light—light is perceived—light is a phenomenon.

JC: Light, though, in this case is a release from time. That's the key because in encountering light or lights, you are always taken out of time. Plotinus has talked about the fact that he only encountered that experience two or three times in his life. It's not suddenly you just latch onto it like you do with an LSD tablet. You're gifted it, but it's clear to me that when he speaks of his moments of grace, that they're both timeless and light filled.

AV: Plotinus in particular, in one extraordinary passage, refers to seeing the spiritual sun and the sun rises. It's an extraordinary passage, that is simultaneously the experience of timelessness. Timelessness in the sense of transcendence. And that is really the dynamic that we're talking about here. It's a dynamic between being embedded in and manifesting in time on the one hand. And on the other hand, being open to and gifted with timelessness.

JC: Yes, absolutely. I recall reading about solar time corresponding to solar mind, alluding to the idea of a light being applied to one's thought process. I remember that vaguely. And I think that Plotinus is particularly apt—I don't see it in Plato, but Plato was a different character in terms of his process. He alludes to it of course. He does allude to it very much so in some of those great dialogues, but you never get the sense that he's been there. You only get that sense that you're referring to.

AV: Because he's speaking the language of the Mysteries—his characters are—he's alluding because that's the language of allusion. Plotinus is different because he's offering exposition, but Plato's work is in the form of dialogue with allusion and symbolism and ellipses and it's there, but it's not there in quite the same way. Then again, what we can say is that in many respects, we're all explorers and we're explorers not only of the geographic reaches of the world, but ultimately, explorers of the terrain that exists between time and timelessness.

JC: I agree, and that's perfectly expressed by the paradise garden in that it's a geographic space that's been reconstructed in the mind of the narrator, which refers to something that was geographic in the twelfth century that might not have necessarily been filled with all this knowledge that I had placed upon it, but my writers, our writers say that garden which King Roger built was a metaphor for his deep and avid desire to contain all the knowledge of the world as he did in his library system in Palermo, and he invited philosophers and people to come and live there—people like that great explorer. What was his name?

He wrote a wonderful book. I've forgotten his name now, but he became a man that actually then set about and fashioned a map of the world as big as this on silver for King Roger. And that again is another metaphor of the garden. Bring the world into your study. So my sense is that by building it, a paradise garden, and putting into it all of thought. This endeavor is entirely conceivable. because in the sixteenth century, as I allude to in the book, an individual built theaters of memories throughout in Venice in particular, and persuaded the King of France to build one. He was alluding to the fact that you could put thought into physical space—thought. And that's fascinating. That thought could be imposed upon a place. Well now, of course I know that with Aborigines, they impose thought and a judgment if you'd like via a Dream, which is a story in landscape that's always there. They can pick it up and put it back just like those people did in the theater of memory did, and all those fellows in the sixteenth century, so you can see the parallels.

AV: You can see the parallels and you can see the relevance of the theme of earthly paradise—the revelation of timelessness in time. And that might be a good place to draw our conversation to a close.

JC: Yes, I think that's a good thought. There's timelessness in time as the chrysalis is in the cocoon—and it breaks out and it butterflies. That sense of the golden globe, a construct of time, but it's golden because we're fascinated with what we see in time. Right? The world? But inside that is this chrysalis, which is the spiritual nature of that [which is] being nurtured within the great globe.

Fourth Conversation:

KNOWERS

JC: We emerged from our wonderful mornings of discussion to ultimately arrive at the sense of the value of, let's call it megalithic cultural life—and we acknowledged that these places and artifacts and constructs are enmeshed in a spiritual life of this time, whether it's associated with stars and moons and order in the Heavens, so to speak, and that is then spread through culture in terms of practice, which is religious. The important thing now is saying we're addressing the issues of the material aspect of the megalithic culture as we piece together the certain reality we hope that might be valid. We also need to address and be open about what sort of spiritual life can that enact and that's why I'd thought we discuss it today.

AV: The starting point that you're posing is megaliths—which can be represented by large stones, like menhirs, and in miniature by something as small as churinga stones. Megaliths of course exist across Western Europe and also, of course, you might be referring to the stones of Australia. I suspect that when you say "megalithic," you mean the megaliths of Western Europe and coming to terms with what their meaning is, precisely because they are in the West itself. And in the most Western part of both France and the UK, Ireland, Scotland, especially along the coast, they are present still, yet they are overlooked. They are ignored. They exist and they exist pretty much as they have for thousands of years untouched. But what do they mean? How do we incorporate their meaning into a contemporary context? I think that's what you're talking about and that's a good question. And it ties in more broadly with what spiritual light is in the first place. What would you have to say about what megaliths have to offer us in an era in which technology has reached such sophistication and machinery is so sophisticated and complex and distracting? What do megaliths offer us? What is it that we can draw either from Aboriginal or from European ancient cultural traditions or artifacts?

JC: I think that gets to the root of what I'm trying to express – and I hope with your help, to tease out that sense that ultimately all the work that's done on megaliths at the academic level or scholarly level is still confined by certain realities tied up with geometry, mathematics, and a kind of vague understanding that these places might have some embedded knowledge that we're not privy to, which is quite right and I respect. But the problem of course is that the people doing the investigation of these places are largely social scientists, people who have come out of a certain kind of discipline—archaeology, astroarchaeology, all of the sciences that have popped up over the last century—and they are still driven by a certain kind of empiricism that they are looking for to ascertain and confirm within what they're doing. So the site itself ultimately becomes an experimental venue rather than a cultural venue. And that's what I think is often missing in the general dispersion of these ideas in books and things like that because they don't want to get into spirituality. I was discussing it with a scholar and I could see he didn't want to go there, because he thought that would go outside of the parameters he set up through his academic background. And so where I mentioned the idea of a spiritual life, inside that endeavor and how one accesses it, that strikes me as the core of the question. If we don't understand the principal values behind it, we'll always only be reduced to measurements and signs or fences around it to keep out the populace. We are in an age where, as you rightly point out, technology has reached its apogee and we're completely distracted by it. There is also the fact that because religions generally in the West anyway have been declining in their impact on cultural life, except on the fringe where you have Sufism or Buddhism creeping in, which is fine, but it's an importation to a certain extent. Trying to fill a vacuum that Christianity has left in the wake of its exoterism, I suppose. And so the spiritual life in the broadest sense is either deeply pious and filled with the notion of piety, or it ends up in a fringe area where people are eccentric in their relationship with spiritual life because they find they can pick up brand new techniques from Buddhism, and in particular techniques from Tibetans, all of which is valid, but they're ultimately grasping at something that is of another tradition, where what we're talking about in terms of megaliths is still inside our tradition, it's just very early, and the spiritual life that has inherited that, my sense is, has an absolute validity for the twenty-first-century man if you'd like—that he or she can find through access to the megalith. I use it broadly, as you know. They are able to partake of a certain kind of spiritual reality which they've probably felt reluctant to do inside the context of Christianity or that they didn't want go to Buddhism, or they didn't want to become Sufis, but they are still grasping for some meaning on the societal and personal level, so that's the thought—I thought, well, what is it about the spiritual life that is valid to the people of an ancient tradition that we can look at or re-look at today? And that's what I thought was worth while exploring with you. So, I'll ask you your thoughts about that.

AV: The first thing I would say about megalithic sites and stone cairns like those at the top of the great hills overlooking half of Ireland, is that those are situated in very particular places. They don't appear just anywhere. They are in very particular places and they require us to go to those places, which are wild. They are in nature. Sometimes you're walking through herds of sheep in the high hills. Sometimes you're walking through forests. But there are certain characteristics—certain aspects of those places. Sacred springs, holy wells—that speak from a very specific place—a specific area with certain kinds of characteristics that you can begin to identify and come to read like a language. And so it's not that, from my perspective, there's an opposition between what I call indigenous Europe and traditions from elsewhere or traditions that arise elsewhere because what we're talking about is really about reading the language of nature, which is something that one can do elsewhere, but what I'm specifically pointing towards is that these monuments, these places, exist in Europe. And they are *of* Europe and that's significant. By experiencing them, by hiking back to one in the high hill country, you're in some way contacting an entirely different way of seeing the world because you're literally, as well as figuratively, leaving the modern world behind and entering into another way of relating to the natural world—the natural world not just as an assemblage of biology and geology, but as spiritual reality. Now Tibetan Buddhism, for example, offers particular disciplines and particular practices that may very well be helpful in understanding what we're talking about in a different way and in a deeper way. And that's fine as far as I'm concerned. There's no inherent opposition between them.

JC: Inclusiveness is what you're talking about too—that sense that all could be included in that great term we call the spirit.

AV: That's right and the other thing is that because exoteric Christianity, you could say literalist Christianity, is so far removed from what we're talking about, it becomes necessary to find our way back to deeper connections to the natural world, often times through other traditions. It's why you went to live among and engage with Australian Aborigines. It's necessary to do that in order to understand more deeply the nature of Australian sacred places. There's no other way. At the same time, what people often don't realize is that actually there are sacred sites in Europe as well and we're just not aware of them. We're not familiar with them.

JC: Thousands too.

AV: Thousands, tens of thousands. It's an extraordinary inheritance.

JC: It's a Dreaming landscape—as we understand Aboriginal Dreaming, but in this case the Dreaming is gone. We have to find it. You'd have to find it where it's not—and that's the interesting thing. We're talking about megalithic culture—like I was talking about the Torajans lost their capacity to write letters because they got washed away by a flood and they lost—in a sense lost language. And the way that the megalithic cultures are no longer present, they are no longer with us, so we're having to renew ourselves to the point where we're extracting new information from old artifacts, and that's where the spiritual life seems to me is buried in those stones, the rocks, and the landscapes, but we've lacked the specific tools to engage in that landscape outside of the normal popularization of Druidic activity and getting dressed up in costumes on certain days of the years, etc., which is perfectly fine, but I'm talking about something entirely different. That the spiritual life, at say Stonehenge, would've been rich—a tapestry of cultural activity that brought forth from the alignments and the specific arrangements if you'd like of nature at a given time of the year—that resulted in deeply spiritual significance. And that had a powerful effect on the culture to keep them together—keeping their stories together, keeping them figuratively speaking one shared language. Watch in the film how eagerly the Aborigines looked at the ritual that was being performed in front of them. They'd probably seen it fifty times but it's still terribly important to engage in that ritual activity in order to find a spiritual message. And even though at the end of that documentary, the Aborigines say "Well, it's all over, you can go home," a surprisingly abrupt remark after three days of heavy-duty work on a ritual. But ultimately, that's perfect because they're just saying we've enacted the spiritual life in a certain kind of way—think about it, but we're not going to say it. It's all right, but that's how they are: so people would say that's pretty sort of matter of fact, but Aborigines are matter of fact. They don't have that kind of courtesy that we would have. They would never say to you "thank you," if you did something for them. The word doesn't exist. Why thank somebody? But we have a close relationship, I would do whatever I can and if I've got $2, that $2 is yours. So the word "courtesy" is a European construct, I very quickly realized, so I understood I had to think differently, in Aboriginal terms. People would say, "They didn't thank you, Jim." I would say, "Why would they?" We were engaged in something between us that doesn't involve a thank-you note. And so in a sense, I'm saying that that spiritual life, which we're talking about in the stones, we have to find a way to articulate it. And that ultimately comes down to the creative environment in which we like to place our souls and relationships and this material. That's why I make such a to-do about language. How important language is and how important words are, what they actually mean, and what their etymology is, because you then slowly but surely are releasing imagination into the world that we're pursuing, which is the spiritual light and my sense is that the spiritual light of these people both past and present is determined largely by processes—what's the word?—preambles, that are consistent right through the whole millennial history. They're not grafting a new thing on. People say, well, Christians, they brought asceticism into the world. Of course, that's patently not true—we know that. But in a sense, it was clearly an important aspect of the spiritual life. It was a part of the language of the life—the ascetic life and I write about that a lot. I write about the ascetic life and even to Christians, they get quite upset—they say, "Well, it's not like doing good." I say, "No, it's got nothing to do with good works." In fact, it's outside that preserve of good works, which you're comfortable with, so that the ancient life that we're talking about and its relevance today—it seems to me that we have to, in a sense, find a way of expressing what it would be like to be megalithic. All my life as a writer, I wanted to answer the question, "What is it like to be an Aborigine?" The empathy factor is quite important in that relationship and if you're a good writer, you can embark upon that journey, but that's the journey that I'm talking about in terms of the spiritual life. Aborigines might know about ritual, initiation, pain, loss of identity, loneliness, being subincised, damaged, introduced to esoteric material at a certain time in the ritual activity. Kind of like a university for those young boys of nine, ten, eleven, when they go passing into the process of learning the spiritual life of their culture. And it seems to me that also is a part of what megalithic culture has yet to address in terms of writing about it. It's all of what we've discussed, and the challenge is to make it relevant to the twenty-first century and to people who are all yearning, and all of them as you rightly know, say, "Well, I respect trees. They've got spirit, and I love the landscapes." They go into these kind of wonderful joyous paeans about "I worship nature." That's the keyword. I worship nature. I don't need to worship a God or I don't need to go to church, etc., because I've got nature at my foot, but they actually don't explore beyond that. They have no sense of well, what is the language nature is going to teach me about the spiritual life? And that's where I've seen this discussion and the work that you're going to do is going to lead to addressing our inheritance.

AV: What is that you would say about the Dreaming and about your experiences living with Aborigines? Working with Aborigines during that, especially with that generation of men like Big Bill Neidjie was his name [d. 2002, a Kakadu Aboriginal elder, the last native speaker of that language]. You had the good fortune to know such people, sometimes called men of high degree. They're initiates within that tradition—a tradition that goes back tens of thousands of years. So what did you draw from them that could be of value or help for somebody in the modern world looking at, say, a megalithic site?

JC: I think that's where we have to actually resuscitate concepts that most people find difficult to talk about publicly or indeed to address. And I do, when I talk, bring them up. And actually the response is usually very good, because someone has broken the ice, so to speak. But I would say, take just the example of prayer. Why is prayer so important? People will say, "Oh, well it's a way to say hello to God and say thank you very much for fulfilling my outstanding arrangements." They don't necessarily look at prayer—in general, they definitely don't look at prayer as a discipline—a metaphysical discipline, not just a spiritual one. I say things like, "Well, consider asceticism." Most people just can't understand asceticism. It's outside their periphery. Why do people live in monasteries and not engage with the opposite sex and basically live an hermetic life? It's very hard for you to get across to modern people that ascetics actually are practicing a very particular discipline, which affects you right now because that monastery's functioning isn't a part of the spiritual machinery of our time. And if it's not functioning, then there's an empty shell. The living monastery, I always say, is the cog, latching onto other cogs, throughout Europe, through the monasteries and for that matter in the mystics along the Nile River, etc. These people are functioning for us in the spiritual life. You might think of them as living in sheds or whatever. I say, "You've got to stop thinking like that. Don't think about these people as being escapees from real life." That's the other line that people use is: "Why don't they engage and do good works?" I say, "They are doing good works, but it's not good works that you're talking about. It's another form of good works." It's about refining sensibility. It's about refining language. It's about refining activity so you have asceticism, and you have prayer. And you have solitude and you have silence and you have a lot of things that entail the practical life of a monk or a nun that to outsiders seem like just a waste of time, because they don't have any valid understanding of where they go because we've lost that knack. And so that the megalithic culture seems to me, if it's brought into our world as a valid expression of the spiritual life, it allows one in fact to have a better, a cleaner canvas because it's actually not tainted by Christianity or anything else. You say, what's prayer? It's Christian. No, it's pre-Christian. No, it's also Pagan, and let's get back to that aspect of prayer. And slowly find the language that gives good expression to this new form of thinking that comes out of ancient rocks—that's the new modernity that I was alluding to.

AV: So you can see practices that entail a life in solitude and prayer within a Christian context that is not only Christian?

JC: Absolutely.

AV: And that's part of what we're talking about broadly in terms of spiritual life. It's not good works in the sense of constructing a building for somebody. Although, there's nothing against that, but it's a different kind of good work. But how does that connect to what you learn from the Aborigines?

JC: That's where I've been and come from. And it took me many years to reframe the questions that I asked Aborigines because as I went into it, I learned more, and so therefore you're having to revise whatever your simplest question was three or four years before or whatever. But ultimately I came away with a sense that Aborigines, when we were able to dialogue, saw things like prayer in a similar but different way to us. They wouldn't pray in the kind of formal way that Christians do and I think Buddhists do as well. For Aboriginals, prayer was largely a retreat from the real world. What they call real—small r— is entering into a domain where their spirit and even their soul perhaps was enlarged and enhanced. And that could only come about by engaging in ritual. Ritual seems to me the missing link in all of the discussions. They talk about ritual in a Catholic sense, but really it's just a kind of formalism that occupies the space for an hour and a half. It's not the genuine sense of the ritual as we noticed in the Aboriginal ceremony when they were throwing the fire over the guys, getting burned, and that ritual had a very different sense about it than a priest holding up the wafer and saying da da da and performing, which is no longer a ritual *per se*. It's just an act to give some sense to why people are in there in the first place. And that engagement physically between the man, the land, and the myth—to me is the bedrock of the spiritual life for Aborigines. So you can't detach one from the other. You can't say, "well, go away and pray." You say, "What's prayer?" He says, "Well, you go away and dance." Yes. That is prayer. Or when they walk along the cave wall of the great serpent Jarapiri, and they pray. They pray all the way along that thing. They've got their prayers. They know the wall. But nobody would ask that question about Aborigines. They wouldn't say, "Well, they're a prayerful nation." And probably Native Americans—they wouldn't answer the question by speaking of a Native

American prayer for nature or whether they practice asceticism. Yet yes, they do. Young boys, you off to the bush for three months. Survive. Take a boomerang and a spear or whatever, and you live there and you'll be depressed, and you'll be distorted, and you'll be hated. But you'll come back a man. So that asceticism is embedded in the ritual construct of becoming an adult, if you like. It's not the asceticism that we understand in a Christian sense or in a Buddhist sense where they sit for a very long time and meditate. So when you can get those things working in your head from an ancient culture, then you can see "Oh, there is logic to this." Asceticism, prayer, solitude, silence are the four truths if you like of the ascetic life. I think that people would respond to that. I do think they will respond because it allows the freedom to say, "Well, I used to love nature but now I'm beginning to know why I love nature and I'm going to put a little more into it in terms of my prayer." Even to pray—to pray—how many people pray? It's considered to be a religious act rather than a genuine evocative act. And I find when I do discuss these things, which I inevitably do in public space, people respond quite well. They may get over the shock of it. You explain how things work. How an ascetic lives and what it gives to that person. Because that's the other thing. People will ask the question, "Well what is it that a spiritual life is going to give you?" It's quid pro quo stuff. I always say, "I can only tell you my experience with great spirituals is that what they offer is their presence and their presence is so powerful that it in itself is a prayer. And you've rubbed up against the prayer. And you walk away from it knowing what an extraordinary moment that has been in your life to rub up against that prayer in the presence in the condition of that man, that life, his soul, his going against the grain of his culture perhaps." And if that's teased out in a right way, not in an indoctrinating way, you will find people to respond to it—my sense is that people want that. They don't want Christianity—it's old forms. They can't stand Abrahamic culture, a vindictive law, an eye for an eye. Ditch that. Ten Commandments—well, they were relevant in their time, but I don't know if they've got much going for them now. They can find all sorts of excuses to erase Christianity from their psyche even though it's embedded in them, because they're people. So that's what I wanted to ask you—how you thought—and probably it's just stimulating thinking about it—but the sense that there is a way forward as a creative writer. As you engage in this material, to bring forth from it, its essential, primordial metaphysic, that is spiritual. It's not just an interesting set of concepts. It touches you deeply and people can be touched by it. And therefore we start to frame the vocabulary of expression of a megalithic spirituality. It hasn't been done. That's why we're talking about it. I tried to do it in *Return to the Dreaming* and you'll see how I've worked it through. Coming to grips with landscape, voice, ritual, and the Dreaming itself—the myth. Blending them all together as a journey back along this timeline over the space to become who I am, and it ends in a rather beautiful way too. That's what I'm talking about. And I think that is what you understand and I think you probably feel was not so much the missing link, but the thing you hadn't arrived at yet in your research, and your studies are just a clear intimation it's there.

AV: That's why I'm broaching the question of working with and being with Aboriginal people, because it seems to me analogous that there's much to be drawn from your experience as a highly literary sensibility drawing on and coming to understand that other perspective that's so ancient. What we're not talking about here necessarily, although it's possible, but I don't think we're necessarily only talking about Paganism as it's usually understood. It's also a question of how we are in relation to our own cultural pasts and our own roots in Western Europe. I think what's happened in the last several hundred years is on the one hand, we've developed coming out of Western Europe, extraordinary technological prowess. But at the same time, to a large extent, we lost our own roots. And there's a degree to which in order to recover that, we need to come to terms with the significance, the meaning of our own history and our own roots. And that's what I'm talking about. And part of that is what you're referring to as the spiritual life, which is different than religious life. Religious life has to do with particular social aspects, and what we're talking about can manifest itself in religious life, and often it does, as you're referring to, in terms of manifestations, whether it's ritual or physical. But the spiritual has to do with the inner life, and that's where the challenge that you're posing lies. And with regard to myth, something that we've referred to before, mythology is conceived often as separate category from literature. It's a separate category in which we're looking at the misguided beliefs of misguided people from the past.

These kinds of artificial constructs, as it were, that they "believed in" in their benighted state, and of course that kind of perspective cuts us off from our own collective cultural origins. Materialist or literalist beliefs that automatically reject mythology cut us off from meaning. And so a lot of what we're talking about in terms of the relative disorientation and disconnection of contemporary European humanity either in Western Europe or in the islands, or for that matter, in North America or in Australia or elsewhere—the loss of roots can only be ultimately restored by going back and understanding in a deeper way the literary and mythological expressions of spiritual reality and that's where what you're talking about and writing about in terms of your experiences with Aborigines may be helpful. When Aborigines tell a story of the meaning, what are they telling the story of?

JC: That's a point I think I make in that little essay I gave you. I often use the word *mythos* because I want to break out of that sense that, as you say, words like "myth" are contaminated by pejoratives, so if you use the word "mythos," you break away. Immediately if you can get language to do something it's not used to doing, it arrests people in their reading process. Even words like "shaman"—everybody has a preconceived notion of a shaman and that's it. We don't actually know that a man of high degree is not a shaman, but he manifests the qualities of a high degree—that putting him into a place where language comes into play. Where ritual comes into play. It's not all about getting high on a drug and running around exalted. But that's the perception, so I think one has to relook at the way language is used in the relationship to the expression of these ideas, and also to have a sense that—with Aborigines in particular—it necessitated me going back and looking at the way their language was arranged on the page in terms of the words as best as they could be translated, but literally translated, not creatively translated, which is another dimension there too. But when you see the way words are placed on paper, and the writing that's attached to the expression, because that's very important—like Gregorian chant. Ladadada. People said it was useless but it's actually a very finely expressed form of rhythm that gets to the bones. I don't know if you notice how exact those young Aboriginal men were when they danced. They all landed exactly at the same time together. There was very little rehearsal or choreography, but they got it right because they've got the words in their mind that bring them into that relationship. I know it sounds so strange, but I think that's where to look, at the way language is used in relationship to ritual. That is something that nobody has properly investigated. It's in that parameter that the spiritual life is embedded. It's just that it's not embedded the way we are familiar with it. It's hard enough to break with your own culture, but it's even harder to rebuild another in your mind that gives meaning. And ultimately, I thought that the issue of why one must address a spiritual life and the idea of megalithic cultures as a modern issue is that it does allow people the opportunity, as you rightly point out, to go back to roots. But secondly, it's the one way that's probably left now in this day and age, to go back to meaning. Because meaning in essence is the ultimate expression of any ritual activity. You come away with meaning in your body. And that's something that people just don't address because they don't understand what meaning is in context to the passage of spirituality or numen. Numen in voice. Numen in language. Numen in fate. Numen in sweat. Numen in the construct on the ground as we saw in Aboriginal ritual. Numen in megalithic stones at Stonehenge. All of those things—they are actually all together like cogs in a wheel, they move and they shuffle and they release energy for example. The cogs of the spiritual life are there to release a certain kind of energy into being and that is something that sounds materialist at one level, but actually it's the only way people understand today if you can capture certain terms like I've just done—you say, yes, I can understand—it's got meaning. But ultimately you want people to understand that to embrace a cultural expression like this, it doesn't mean that you suddenly become someone loopy, with a clover in your hair kind of way, that's not what I'm getting at. That absolutely needs to avoided. Nor does it mean you have to give up being a Christian or Buddhist—they're the conventional means by which you've expressed yourself since childhood or that you've practiced and developed. But you can live more than one life spiritually. I can have Hermes on the wall and Christ next to him. Doesn't bother me. I see them both all in the same terms of numen. And Aborigines do too. They go to church on Sunday. Listen to the prayer and haven't said a word. And they go back and they're back in the Dreaming and chatting away. I asked Mick about it. He said, "Well, I can do that. I can go to two places at the same time that are beautiful." And I never forgot, in my book, I don't know if you ever read my novel *Toby's Angel.* You must've seen it. Well, the character, Ray, from Rafael the Angel, also included an allegory of golden fleece, by the way. Tobias and the angel. He said—the angel said, "I just go up and down in my mind." And when people read that, they laugh and go, what a strange expression. I said because an angel has the capacity to rise up and live in that domain. But he can come down here too. He's going up and down. He's not going anywhere in life on the road because Toby said, "Well where do you want to go?" He said, "That doesn't matter to me. I go up and down in my mind all the time. That's my destination and journey." And it seems to me that that's the life of a megalithic man in his spiritual life. That needs to be worked on, because we haven't done enough work in that area yet. We have a palimpsest here: we're trying to play with ideas that are in our mind—almost a morphosis fashion, but we're trying to dig deeper and find out why and what. That's my sense of the spiritual life in relationship to this exploration of the megalithic.

AV: What we're talking about is primordial in the sense that when you go to a cairn high in the mountains, when you go to a holy well, which to reach you have to first of all find where the entrance is—maybe through a guide. Find the path. Then make your way along the path. And then you recognize it immediately when you're there because there are signs and offerings. Those are primordial places—the top of a mountain overlooking the entire landscape, a spring where water is coming out of the earth pure and immediate, and you can look into the spring and see the darkness, out of which the water is coming. And it's pre-mythological. It's not necessarily that there's a story that's attached to it. Although there often is. But, the kinds of places we're talking about are primordial and archetypal—going to the top of the mountain. Going in the cave. Crawling through—a cairn is not just a pile of stones. It actually has passageways like birth canals in it as long as it's still standing, that is, through which you crawl. Crawling through a birth passage into this area in which you can then sit or stand. And that too was primordial. It's crawling through this passageway into a different world. So what we're talking about is in some sense, pre-mythological, meaning prior to language, prior to fiction or poetry, but which can be given an expression through those things. And that then leads to thinking about the creation of literature as the creation of mythology—mythology not just as what exists frozen in the past, but in some sense, as something that can reach expression in new ways today. What would you have to say about the role of literature in terms of expression of the primordial?

JC: It's a question that I grappled with for most of my writing life. Feeling I think that literature has a role to play in primordial expression and I think that primordialists of the past—people like Guénon and Coomaraswamy, while they didn't necessarily address language in the way we're talking about, possibly hadn't reached the point of understanding how linguistics and language essentially are a part of the spiritual life—it's like a graft. I grappled with it for a long time and it got to the point where as a writer, there was no alternative but to grasp the nettle of finding new expression within the constraints of the English language and its rules and regulations so to speak. But nevertheless, find a way to make more vivid the metaphoric life of language. Does that make sense? Make more vivid the metaphoric life of language. As you know, in the last 150 or last 180 or 200 years, the reductionism of industrial life in England and later on elsewhere, flattened out language to erase and extinguish its richness, so language became more efficient at doing what it does because it conveys information quickly. Give me that flat. Give me that wrench bucket. On and on and on it goes. And so the language—language as hyperbole—has been lost. And one of the things I used to love about Aborigines when they do those dances they do, was they get so excited and so angry if you didn't say it the right way. And then they'd say "I'm the one that puts this show on. Who is he?" An act of hyperbole. People would say that's just boasting. It's not. He's saying, "I'm the essential ingredient to make this thing come alive. I deserve recognition as much as the song itself." Wow, I love that. It's just the sense of power that's in voice and when they discuss these, particular in those ritual environments, they get very heated with one another. They're going to knock each other out. They've allowed their chests to ventilate language in a way that changes them from being an ordinary Aboriginal that's just coming off the back of a truck to somebody that's already coming in touch with the other, and that's why it's essential to paint people up. Put all that stuff in. Redden their face. Change their whole appearance, because they're already moving out of the normal space of life into the surreal, into the super-real space, and that I'm sure is an essential part of the megalithic way as well. But it's the sense that they have very particular mechanisms for accessing the spiritual life, which then translate into all sorts of ramifications for society, ethics, love, emotions, morality, danger. All the things that go on—I've never ever had a sense that Aborigines didn't have a high ethical stance in everything they did. Far more than we did. So there are a lot of times that they say, "You can't do that." No, you can't do it. It's against the culture. But we wouldn't do that, we'd tolerate the difference in the terms of ritual—it's all right. If he wants to kick up his heels now, it's fine because it's personal expression. They don't like that. It's got to be straight on the line. That's the way it's been for 2,000, 10,000, 20,000 years. That quality evokes in most twentieth, twenty-first-century people a sense that their freedom is being taken away. And that's the key to it. People think if I can't give my own expression to this, then I'm no longer a free person, and to overcome that is one of the difficult things of making relevant a megalithic spirituality if you'd like. Because people would say I don't want to go back there. I don't want to sit for an hour and then say the Jesus prayer or whatever. I just want to pick this stuff up as I want to, like I do with this machine in my hand. But that's where I think literature in the old primordial sense has some role to play. And it has to do with how you use language. How you play with it as I suggested in that piece we read last night. That there is an element of play in all ritual. I think here of the book by Johan Huizinga, *Homo Ludens*, arguing that most activities that man engages in are an elaborate play, ludic—that play is an essential part of our souls and modern man is—I don't know what the Latin word is for efficiency, *Homo efficiensis* is a modern construct, for man was never like that in the past. He liked to play. He liked to have his festivals throughout the year and the ritual because that gave meaning to life. And the temple gave meaning to life. And the megalith gave meaning to life and that I'm sure will resonate with the modern mind that doesn't want to revisit Augustine or a couple of texts by great Buddhists. They wouldn't want to go there because it's too serious for them. So my sense is that that's where the spiritual life inside this new envelope we were discussing will challenge a writer. It'll challenge you. I started it. I did start it and I've gone a way along the path, and I feel *Palace of Memory*, which I shared with you, was essentially about transcendence—having to do with hidden knowledge. It was all about how men find meaning in growing vegetables, feeding a tortoise, getting a philosopher to engage with you among the flamingos in the garden. There's a quite complex interrelationship between nature and ideas in the garden. It's not just a bunch of philosophers wandering around. There's a whole wonderful sequence, which you'll love. There's a Chinese fellow named called Ko Hung comes to town. He gets off the boat at Palermo, and he meets the geographer that I was talking about. And I have him going down to the docks every day to meet people to get new ideas and he draws Ko Hung into King Roger's world and he gets him into the garden. Why? Because Ko Hung comes to the places as an alchemist, but he also comes as an escapee because everybody wants him because he makes gold. But finally because he knows herbs. He knows plants. And there's almost two chapters I think where Ko Hung and what he represents in terms of flowers and plots is absolutely surreal, but I took it from ancient Chinese texts. I didn't make it up. I merely gave it its new dressing in terms of a man who comes from China and ends up in Palermo and becomes a friend of King Roger. And that's sort of language that the writer is going to have to deal with. You have to break down the barriers when you think, "Well, I can't use this because it has historical associations that I can't extract it from." I'm saying you can. You've got to find a way to do it. So I found through a Chinaman—Chinese people, they didn't get much mention in Europe, because there were very few of them. But there were Hindu temples in Alexandria pre-Christianity, because of pilgrims or travelers coming across from India and places like that. People like our friend Plotinus were familiar with Asia in his time—that down the road was a Hindu temple, and there were Hindu priests, and when you talk to people from India, you get different perspectives from life. So the writer today has to draw on that new configuration through language and careful use of metaphor that he wouldn't have done in the past. He would just write on, get the characters moving, get them talking, throw in a bit of patchwork locale, and off you go. I put it in. But it's illusory. It's not there in the modern realist sense. It's put in there—usually within the context there's something going on again underneath the surface of whatever I'm describing in terms like Ko Hung coming into town and when he's buried, I can recall vaguely. They buried him—when they opened the coffin, they found nothing. Just his neatly rolled clothes and his hat. [laughs] He disappeared! In other words, he was an illusion in the first place. You couldn't do that in normal realist literature. You have to find this totally different way of expressing things that's satisfactory enough for young readers to understand, "Oh we're in Palermo." And the Palace of the Normans is down the road, but the Palace that I've created through the paintings on the roof of the churches and things like that. In the book, the character of Roberto goes in there to have a look at it and then he has a complete break, his mind completely loses contact with reality through the images coming down upon him—streaming down these Christic images. He embarks from that point on into the garden. The hardest thing was to find a way to get him into the garden in real time without the readers saying that can't happen. I had to find a way of doing that and I did it by finally putting him in the church of the Palace of Normans, the tessarae and the colors and the light—all of that basically became hallucinatory, if you like; that allowed him to get into the garden and then I was off with the garden at my disposal. So that's what I'm talking about, the way you conduct your images and the way you address your metaphors. You have to create new metaphors. But you have to do it specifically. You're not just going to do it for effect. You want your metaphors to be in the text. You don't want them to be eroded or gotten rid of as in modern language—the idea of a metaphor is very low in the order of writing space, but allegory, metaphor, symbolism—all of those things have to be given a more robust life in contemporary literature from my point of view for this kind of writing to present itself, which allows things like the visitation of the megaliths to come alive. To come alive!

AV: What we're talking about really in part is the renewal of literature through reintroduction of origin, reintroduction of the primordial. It's not that it's artificial—we're not talking about artificially creating some kind of ancient or quasi-ancient tradition. It's about making things new again. It's about renewal in the literal sense of re-new and what's being renewed comes out of nature. It comes out of a new sense of nature and what it means to be human that is somehow also archaic. In some sense, it's both archaic in ancient and it belongs to the future. And it in that sense, what we're discussing is both the origin of culture and the renewal of culture.

JC: Absolutely, and I think that the issue of literature as you earlier expressed is, while it sounds quite facile because it's the sort of the thing that people say, "That tree speaks to me." What they don't quite understand is that the language that we're employing when we say, "nature speaks to us," to me that's an immensely challenging linguistic problem because it is trying to attach the idea that nature has a language that we understand in the real sense and the primordial sense. But that we have failed to recognize that the language we think nature is speaking to us is not the language we think it is. And so from a writer's point of view, when I say you have to refine your metaphors, you have to change the way you put your metaphor together, not for effect. You've got to be very careful that the metaphor you create is embedded in a real sense of its rightness. And that way, if I was to say, "Well, when we open up the leaf of a tree, we measure it mentally. We know its shape roughly, and we accept all of those accoutrements of a leaf as being a leaf." We don't then look at the leaf any more in that. We won't say, "Well, what is the meaning of leaf? What is its leaf-ness?" And that's the key to this kind of writing. That you're trying to release through metaphor and the other things that you're using—the timelessness of the sentence. I told you about that a few days ago when I said the sentence has to be timeless—time has to be removed from it in order for that sense to become more spiritually compressed. Then when you look at the leaf and say, "How does that leaf-ness affect me?" The only way you can do that is through a new metaphor. A new way of writing. You just can't say the leaf is green, it grows on trees, it falls, it's deciduous, it's shaped like—that's irrelevant, because what I want is leafness. That's where the genuine literary process comes into play and that's the hardest thing. And you have to be intellectually well-equipped, but you have to be spiritually well-equipped because you're grappling with the leaf-ness as an expression of deep primordiality and you—and when you write it and you get it, you got it. You know when you've suddenly hit a metaphor in those poems in which I gave you yesterday. You'll find there a range of startling metaphors carefully thought, worked, constructed in order to break the rhythm of the line, the sensibility, the verbosity, you feel like, so that as the reader, you say right, "Where am I now?" I'm saying you're in the Dreaming. I'm trying to take you into the Dreaming through a poem, so that you no longer see the real world outside. I want this poem to be your only reality for the given time that you're in it. And that's different than just the normal literary process, which as we talked about earlier, has got the gap between it and the Real. And one's trying to find that return to primordiality in language and that's why etymology and Greek and Latin, for us at least, Sanskrit for somebody like yourself who has contact with that ancient language, you go back to that time and time again. I've got a Latin dictionary. I don't speak Latin, but I know it. It's in my blood. I did study it, so I know how to construct it, but I can't say that I can ever read fully or speak Latin. I'd love to do it. That's the same with Greek. Those are our tools and so I think one has to—if we're getting to that new language in literature, which expresses the primordial, which expresses the megalithic culture, you have to go to those extreme limits to find that language. I'd be very careful about the way it's being used down to every color. Every nuance. Every adjective. Hemingway never liked adjectives, and said they should never be used. But actually, they're there, and you have to occasionally use them because they do have an effect, so I'm never going to take that austere kind of posture myself. One has to allow adjectives to creep in occasionally because they're beautiful words too. So that's what I mean when I say a spiritual life within this context relies on this new journey—old journey, new journey. Back into the way language constructs itself and that comes from leaf-ness and finding a way to get the leaf literally to do its job on us, and that I think will release this kind of power that Aborigines and the ancient peoples of prehistoric Europe would have understood, and made it understood because they had two languages. They had their day language and their secret language. I remember telling you about the way that they have two languages and sometimes three to express certain realities. We have got to have that sense of a double or treble language and that's what I did in the book *Palace of Memory*, where the king has a name and he has his body. That was a deliberate articulation of the idea that Name, or Logos, if you like, must be in a sense attuned for its own sake. Not just that's King Roger down there, he's rotting. His name is intrinsic to his essential soulness, and adjacent to but separate from flesh, so again that sense of how do you make this language that we're talking about work in strange oddities like that, or Ko Hung wandering through all these herbs, and creating a whole new space intellectually and spiritually in a garden, who was dedicated to European virtues and things like that. So as a writer, you asked earlier what advice you'd give to a young writer—it is the essential need to do a lot of spade work early in your career when your ideals are not congealed in terms of reading broadly across cultures and understanding the contiguity between the two, or three, or five, and being happy with it. It might take you years to actually acquire it. I was thinking about this conversation in which we were chattering away about Plato and Plotinus and this woman who overheard us was wondering, where am I? This is not a normal world. This must be that other language. Right? For her it was probably a breath of fresh air because she'd never heard this kind of talk, but we are so confident in that world not as scholars or as academics or whatever, but because we've actually taken it in our body. That it's the leaf-ness of the culture that is now a part of our construct so when you and I talk or when I talk to our friends, they always say well, you bring so much history to the table and you always know where to find things. I say yes, only because it's in my blood. It's no longer something that I picked up from a book.

AV: That's the other end of the spectrum of what we're talking about in some respects, but they're connected. On the one hand, being in the natural world, being in a primordial place, coming to understand that anew for the first time in that archaic way is where we started, but where we're concluding is also the importance of culture, and culture as the summation, as drawing from what's gone before and expressing that in a second language—a language which is not that of efficient, bureaucratic, orderly, mechanical speech, but rather a secret language, which requires a deeper understanding and it requires all of that cultural familiarity in order to be able to work within it and so on the one hand, you have primordiality. And on the other hand, you have the summation of cultural knowledge that you're drawing from, and both of those are actually necessary. By talking about the first, we weren't suggesting a kind of Rousseauian posited life as a blank slate in nature, but rather on the one hand, going back to origins, and on the other hand, not rejecting but fully understanding and absorbing the totality to the extent one can of one's cultural inheritance. And both of those things are necessary.

JC: Yes, are you conscious of that distance of yourself from other people in the way that I've expressed it?—that there are certain people, like you and I, who are knowers rather than watchers? I expressed in the trilogy that we are knowers. We *were* watchers. We've made it our business to become knowers rather than just watchers. You can be both at the same time, but the watcher is somebody that accepts with due diligence what is being offered, whereas a knower is somebody that says, "But the secret story on the churinga is underneath it and I've got that, you don't." Do you feel that sometimes?

AV: Yes, of course. And perhaps that's a perfect place to end.

JC: [delighted laughter].

Fifth Conversation:

ADVICE TO A YOUNG WRITER

AV: I thought we might talk for a bit about writing and the writer's life, writing not just as something that fills the time as it were, or that provides entertainment, but writing as a living enterprise that requires risks. And I thought you might have some things to say to somebody who is setting out on a life of writing and felt that that was a calling.

JC: Yes, well, I think it's probably quite hard for a young writer today to set out on a course of literature as a way of life, primarily because in part literature has been taken over by commonness. And the commonness, in a sense, has determined the agenda of literature in terms of well-manufactured novels, marketing strategies, and I think has produced the exaggerations that are promulgated on the covers or back covers of books. And I think it must be a bit confusing for a young writer, say 20, 21, 24 or whatever, to begin the process of engaging in literature. I think also that the reasons for engaging literature are not necessarily recognized by those people who want to be writers. They see writing largely as an act of self-expression and that's not discouraged by publishers who quite often say, "Write about your life." Or do something autobiographical because you had a pretty interesting life. That's often been said to me by publishers, and I resisted it, and said, "Look. I'm not writing about me as a writer or writing about my life." For me, the life that I have led is purely incidental to the work. And I don't feel that necessarily one should be celebrated to the extent that readers can read about your life, because I believe that's actively engaging in personality, and I don't think that literature is designed for that. I think it's designed as almost dispassionate engagement with thought, but at a very creative level. And to suggest to a writer what and how they should become writers, I always say, "Look. It'll take you ten years to master the basics of craft." You won't at the stage have an original voice (originary voice) because ultimately, if you started young, you've got very little to say anyway. So, you've got to accept the fact that if you trust in the instinct that you have about your inner life, that will finally become manifest through the active craft, perfection, age, experience, knowledge—the four kind of elements that I think are desperately important to being a writer. So you've got to be patient. Patience is probably the primary virtue for becoming a good writer. It's not about writing books and having them published and receiving fame or notoriety, but rather, in a sense, remaining anonymous. I've always tried to remain kind of a hybrid writer in the sense of not removing myself from the public discourse and occasionally giving lectures and talking and attending writer's festivals as a talker. But having had interviews over the years in magazines and journals — ultimately I found that dissatisfying. Of course I did it when I was younger because I thought it was part of the process of being a writer, but I soon realized that's not what being a writer is about. A writer's anonymity is very important to him and should be important to him because he's much freer if he's anonymous. People say, "Oh, well you didn't write a book like the last one." And that's always been an issue with me that publishers have said to me, "Well, why don't you write another *Mapmaker's Dream* or why don't you write another *Painted Shore*?" And I said, "No. That's not what I'm here for – I'm not here to repeat what I've done. I'm here to explore the possibilities of literature." So my sense is that literature is a profound discipline. And in its best moments, it's aligned to metaphysical thinking. And thought that emerges from that and from the great texts—be they Buddhist or Christian or tribal. But there is an alignment between the great texts and the process of being a modern writer and that has to be acknowledged at the beginning by a young writer. That he won't be able to write purposefully until he has acquired knowledge of and a deep knowledge of whatever texts that he has been drawn to. Because I don't think you have to be drawn to every text. You don't have to be—over everything—as a polymath. Right? We talked about that last night—polymathy. But I think you do have to engage in being a polymath too. I don't think it's just a simple thing of saying, "Well, I'm going to write in a certain kind of way and I've got my voice and I'm going to continue on." Being a polymath is important and I think all the great writers to a certain extent are polymaths or have been polymathic, whether they're

Goethe or whether they're Plato. They're polymaths. They're over a lot of stuff. And that's probably not something that writers today recognize because they're not being brought into that discipline of thinking by their teachers or whatever, and so my sense is that you've got to have that string on your bow—that you're going to think and learn from many disciplines. And the beauty of the mind is of course, that it's allowed to be—it finds the synergies. You don't find them, the mind does and it brings together what seems to be disparate material from one discipline and brings it together to another. And that's the mark of a really refined, creative mind. But you aren't born with it. You have to actually do the hard yards of knowledge acquisition, thought and thinking, and slowly but surely, finding your language which you feel comfortable with as a writer. And pursuing your tasks within that domain, so that's my first thought with regard to a writer's kit bag.

What's in the bag? I always emphasize to younger writers they need to have a journal. Not for your personal ruminations about yourself, but rather ruminations about what you're reading, what you're thinking, and what others are thinking that are informing you. So I have no hesitations with putting in quotes of people as I've been reading as I go along—my books are massive quotes. You can trace the history of my reading through all of the books that I've read, and there's one line here, one line there, so don't feel afraid of drawing your peers, whether they're dead or alive, into your intellectual, spiritual, and imaginative mix. They are there for that reason. I mean all great writers steal from other writers—their thoughts, but they make it new again, and they make it different. I have no illusion that many of my books are filled with material, not taken from somebody else, but being fermented by somebody else in the process of thinking and learning. I think that that helps you to raise your thinking to a level whereby it becomes rather easy to think on paper.

Hard to think on paper when you're young. It takes such a long time to get a sentence sorted and a paragraph sorted, and even a chapter sorted. But when you get older, that becomes much easier. It's very like, I said, a master painter He's got a perfect circle, but he's taken fifty years to get there and I think that a writer has that—that's what he's after. The ability to be his own master in words on the page, and that's probably a nearly alien concept to a young writer or a modern writer. Most books, as you know, are determined by a theme that's pre-established by the writer. Well, I'm going to talk about family abuse in the home or sexual behavior by somebody and that's what I'm going to explore. Autism. You can see all these themes pop up in popular literature, a lot of them are written by women because women seem to have an empathy towards that kind of expression. They do write about those things. Actually, I think many modern writers, men writers, don't write about anything now. When you go back to the early twentieth-century people like Fitzgerald and Hemingway for example, they always had something to say about being a man. Even if it was not overt, whereas in the case of Hemingway, it was quite evident. But you got a sense that their manhood was a part of their writing environment. But today, many writers don't have much of that. I don't know why. I don't mean in the popular masculine sense, but I mean the deep sense of manhood. I haven't been able to answer that question why there's been a kind of blurring of masculine intent within the book, whereas women seem to me, as writers, to have blossomed into that context as female writers. Which is quite a contrast, but males seem to be paler as writers today than they were 40, 50, 100 years ago. So that's one of the areas that I think—and the other problem is of course is that if you talk about issues of spirituality within the context of fiction, it's very difficult for people to accept that this should be in fiction at all. It's something you leave to the theologians or you leave to the New Age people or the Christian pietists, whatever. That fiction shouldn't go there. That's one of the reasons why I wrote *The Deposition* because I thought here's a theme that underpins all of Christian—all of Western thought—outside of the classical era, and yet no writer of today would dare to write about Christ or anything to do with that story and that was the reason I wrote it because I said to myself if I as a writer can't go to that place, then there's something wrong with me—lack of courage. When you talked about courage earlier, courage means that you can address a subject that's become so to speak a cultural cliché, and bring something new to the task. That's why I wrote that book. I felt that if Nikos Kazantzakis could have done it sixty years ago or whenever, with his *Last Temptation of Christ* for example, then it is possible today. But there is virtually no book that uses Christian themes of high order as part of their motif today. It's just gone, because, as we talked about yesterday, most people see going into the

Gospels as basically an act of religious duty rather than active literary duty. And I'm trying to say that the Gospels are a literary track as much as they are a spiritual track ,and that if one can't explore the deeper aspects of the Christ figure, that don't align themselves with conventional views of Christianity—then you've lost that whole kernel of Western life from the creative process.

AV: What I would say is that when you go back to the great nineteenth-century American writers, their work is actually imbued with the language of the King James Bible, for example. Much else. It's not that Melville, for instance, was particularly Christian. He was actually also drawing on heretical thought. He was familiar with Gnosticism and with some fairly unusual intellectual and religious terrain that he incorporated into *Moby Dick*. But he also incorporated Shakespeare. It's a Shakespearean novel. He incorporated his own life—his experience. All of these things are interwoven with this extraordinary language ,and that language is imbued with so much of the overall total inheritance—the full Western cultural inheritance and yet in that time, Melville's *Moby Dick* wasn't recognized for what it actually was. And that's often the case. It's not that unusual to have a truly great book be not recognized. Thoreau famously said he had a library of hundreds of volumes, all of which he wrote himself, and what he was referring to was the fact that he had the copies of the books that didn't sell.

JC: [laughter] I see, yes. That's a lovely thought isn't it? Well, that's right, and people like Poe, for example, developed some work that had a greater effect on the Europeans than it did the Americans of today. I think Poe was never recognized in America to the extent he was regarded by the French particularly, and that speaks to what you're saying.

AV: The other thing that I would say is that we're living in a period in which our own past is eclipsed to a large extent for people who come through either a secondary or higher education experience. They are exposed to their own past to the collective cultural inheritance often in negative terms as colonialism or this or that and the past is labeled as a negative.

JC: That's true.

AV: Or, even more common, is that it's simply rendered opaque. It's in eclipse, in a word and that actually puts someone who is an aspiring writer in a really unusual position in that in some sense, as a rebel, or as an outlaw, you're rediscovering against the current—the value of that cultural inheritance—the meaning of it. I've heard in the hallway and others have told me about offhand rejections of Plato for this reason or that reason and I've read such things as well. But Plato was actually an extraordinary figure and you're not going to understand our cultural inheritance or the toolkit—what goes in the kit bag if you don't understand the dialogues, the conversation, and the cosmology and metaphysics that Plato distilled from the Mystery traditions and brought forth with such a wide-ranging effect. So I think there's a kind of paradoxical sense in which for somebody who's starting out, there's so much to discover and in some sense, you're discovering it by overcoming the educational systems.

JC: Yes! That's true.

AV: You're overcoming it and discovering it as a kind of heretic and there's great power in that. That's where the source of power comes from. Actually—the source of energy comes from that. In some sense, it's an extraordinary and paradoxically positive situation because without that, without that polymathic range and without that knowledge, you have no toolkit. You have nothing. There's nothing there. And deep knowledge is necessary in order to be able to become someone who's an aspirational writer, because we're not talking about somebody who wants to be a scribbler, as Nathaniel Hawthorne said. There are plenty of scribblers. We're talking about somebody who's aspiring—who has great aspiration. And in that case, where do you go? I know because I was actually in a program in creative writing. I had a year in a MFA program and it was one of the top programs in the country. The people that I worked with were quite famous, but did I learn anything from it as a writer? And the answer is not really. Because the life of writing comes from a life of the mind, and from knowing and having that range to be able to draw from and I think the kind of creative writing industry to the extent that it doesn't serve that and encourage that, is not really of particular use for somebody who's a writer. I don't know what your thoughts are on that.

JC: I do agree with you that the fashion to educate young men or women to being writers is not the way to go. But evidently, universities here see it as quite a big cash cow. UQ has a very large creative writing faculty school, which makes a lot of money for the university. Even though UQ is largely science-based as a university, it can't afford to get rid of this program because it's so successful. And that's the irony of it all.

AV: It's successful in a financial sense for the university. It creates a certain industry and there's a value in that. For the industry itself, it employs people and there are customers and products and so on, but what we're talking about is actually a creature of a different type entirely.

JC: I think that's absolutely true, Arthur. The vocation to be a writer is not explored at all by people. I don't think they explore them in those courses either. What is the vocation? And I would have to say it's not dissimilar to the vocation of being a monk—finding something that's rather special to your theme or vocation for living with an absolute discipline. That's what I'm thinking of—trying to say. That the idea that you're writing merely for self-expression is not a vocation. It is merely what it is. But as to vocation—I can remember when I was young and I was probably 22 or 23. I can't remember when I wrote my first short stories, and I took them to a quite well-known Australian writer, Frank Hardy, who was a Marxist and written a very tumultuous novel, which explored high capitalism in the form of a man like Rupert Murdoch. Murdoch's father, or grandfather, was a titan of industry. Murdoch's grandfather took HArdy to court to defend his name. This is back in the fifties, I think. The book *Power Without Glory* was a big novel. It put him in a difficult position. He said he made most of his monies in rubles because the Russians picked it up as being one of those rare things that comes out of a Western country that celebrates Marxism. I had an introduction to him. He was living in Manly, which is in Sydney on the beachfront. And I went to see him and he was living above a fish and chip shop, which was a shock to a 22-year-old—the life of a writer above a fish and chip shop. But I went up there and his wife came to the door and I said, "I'm looking for Frank." She said, "Well you'll find him in the pub." "Oh," I said. "I'll go down to the pub." So I turned around the corner with my manuscript under my arm and went to the pub and he was sitting at the bar. I introduced myself and I said, "It's an unusual place to find a writer." He said, "Oh no. This is where I make my living. I play the horses and this gives me enough money to live and I do it at the bar because I can make a phone call." And I thought, "Wow. This is a man on the edge." He's living his life as a gambler in order to live in a fish and chip shop in order to write Marxist novels. A wonderful life! I said, "Could you read these, Frank?" He said, "Yes I'll read them." And so I waited a month or so and came back to him. I went down to the fish and chip shop and I said, "Well, what did you think Frank?" He said, "You want my advice?" I said, "Yes." He said, "Don't become a writer, don't do it, not because you can't write." He said, "Because it's too hard to be a writer." He suffered court cases, much else. I thought, "Wow, that's a pretty amazing statement to make." I took it on board. And the second thing he said to me—"What is it do you think you've got to say?" That was the other important question he asked me as a twenty-two-year-old. What do you think is important enough to say? I blurted out because I probably hadn't thought of the answer, and I said—and it sounds kind of not pompous, but you know what I mean. I said, "I want to explore the spiritual malnutrition of my time." To this day, that still applies. At 22, it just came out to a Marxist. [laughter] Lovely mix in there and so that's what I said. That's what I want to say as a writer and he nodded and said fine. Didn't mean a lot to him because he probably thought spiritual and malnutrition didn't go together. I many, many years later was at a cocktail party. We had a mutual agent together and I walked up to him and said, "Frank. You probably don't know me, but years ago I was a young wet-behind-the-ears writer coming to see you." And he probably didn't remember me, but I mentioned what he said to me—two things. He said, "It's too hard" and "What have you got to say?" He asked, "Did you take my advice?" I said "No." He looked at me and he said, "Good on you, mate." And that was the end of it. That sense that you had to break through his advice, even though he thought it was good advice, which it probably was for a lesser writer. That it's too hard and you need to have something to say. And I never forgot that. That was coming from a writer who had something to say in his domain as a realist writer. He had a lot of fights with Patrick White. Patrick White is not a realist writer, but was actually able to conjure up realism in the terms of the nineteenth-century explorers, etc. But they had that kind of contretemps going on—one was a Marxist realist. The other was imaginative fiction and literature. So I think that that still remains true to me. And I would say to a younger writer those exact same things—firstly, it's very hard. You've got to be prepared for that. Financial insecurity, emotional discontinuity if you'd like—marriages and all the things that go with it. A writer's life is really singular, but obviously you must have a clear thought about what you want to write about. And I've never forgotten that, so that's the only thing I could say if you're addressing young men and women in that environment. I'd give that story. He ended up above a shop in Elizabeth Bay just where we lived. You went to it —you remember that shop on that corner? He ended up up there. Years later, I went around and saw him again—just reminding you of our circumstance—and I thought this is where you'll end up—above a shop. Obviously fish-and-chips shops were his preferred place of living, and he finally ended up living in a caravan up here. He had a sister, I think, and she said park the caravan in the back. And there's a number of writers in Australia that ended up in caravans. So a young writer should be made aware of it, because if you're not prepared for that risk in life, you're not going to be a writer.

AV: What I would say with regard to that is that the most vital part of it all is actually having a vision. Having a vision, having something that has to be said. I've been subject to the same criticism that you have that—or the same query, which is you can't quite predict what my next book is going to be on. That's because I only write things that I really know need to be written. If it didn't have to be written, if it didn't need to be written to fill a gap, why do it? It's to explore something that otherwise hasn't been explored, but needs to be. If it isn't for that, then what's the point? So the vision—the drive is the most important thing and without that, I don't think there's any point really. That is the point. That's part of the driving force that we referred to earlier as aspiration—aspiring—what you're aspiring to is not driven by something outside you or some kind of external standard. It's the inner need—the necessity. The calling. I think the best word is probably calling. You have a calling that drives you beyond these other things because let's face it. The period we're in now, there are more books published with less readers in the United States than ever in history. Incredible number of books published every year because of self-publishing. Simultaneous to that, the number of readers is diminishing because of technology, but all of that aside, how much of that is really worth reading and has value in the sense we're talking about—aspirational value? Value in terms of guiding or moving—taking readers to an entirely new realm, which is part of what we're doing either in nonfiction or fiction. Or poetry. How many of them are aspiring to that? Well, not so many really. And I think that is the critical thing as to how you make a living. Personally I've thought, were I to do things over again, I might very well learn a trade of some sort, and I've given that advice to people who want to write as well.

JC: Yes, that's a good thought.

AV: Whatever that trade is, I thought electrical work, or carpentry, or something that provides freedom. You make your own hours. Thursday you go and wire up a house and you're done for a little while. Or computer security or whatever it might be.

JC: A geek.

AV: Whatever, that provides—

JC: The wherewithal to live.

AV: The wherewithal to live. Gambling to me doesn't work—for me, that would not be a solution really.

JC: He would have come out of the Depression and the Depression would've been trying to make two pennies out of four, or four out of two, and the horses had a certain romantic association with them. He did it. He made it. It's not that he died of hunger in the end. He died of just being an old man and in the end largely lost from view, because he and his work didn't carry through, but that's the nature of realist writing too.

AV: It's very time specific. Marxism, Communism, that kind of Soviet realism that existed, which was a phenomenon outside the Soviet Union, that is really what you're talking about, it has a certain expiration date stamped in it. And what we're talking about doesn't have an expiration date stamped in it, in that the aspiration is beyond particular timeframes. It's timeless and in that sense, free.

JC: I think that's very true. I often think of—when you look at people of—good examples of the writer's life. I remember people like John of Patmos. A friend of mine went to Greece and she actually said it transformed her really. She couldn't stop writing to say how good it had been. But whatever he was and whoever he was, the idea of writing the apocalypse as a text that stood the test of time. Might not agree with it, but it stood the test of time. It's a mighty, mighty text. And I think a writer should tip his hat to that sort of writing and say well that's the top of the tree of aspirational writing. You need to find these people in your own life experience that might embody this sort of context. My sense is that's also important—that you do find people who you willingly submit your hubris to, you become humble in the light of that man or woman's work. Therese of Avila's *Interior Castle* is a wonderful book. Not many read it, just a few others like us, but it's an enormously important text that will stand the test of time.

AV: Or *Mirror of Simple Souls* by Marguerite Porete.

JC: And I was trying to think of one of those people last night when I said your involvement with—and I wanted to say female writers and I was going to say I should've said to you can you name some of these writers? What's the other woman's name that comes into mind? She's alive, isn't she? That woman that you met in California.

AV: Oh yes, Bernadette Roberts. Yes, another contemporary mystic.

JC: Yes, I remembered her but I didn't remember her name. Those people are there. They're the Team Versluis or the Team Cowan that we look to to pass the ball, or they pass the ball to us, or whatever. So don't feel afraid of the deep influences that are out there. How many writers say to you, "Well I don't read other people's work because I don't want to be influenced." You've heard it. I've heard it. [much laughter]

AV: Oh yes, it's very common.

JC: It's the *tabula rasa*. I'm free. The palimpsest I'm there to be scratched upon.

AV: Yes, the blank slate, a state of nothing, to be inscribed upon and of course, what you end up then is with a blank slate.

JC: It was the same with the potter who you met, Richard, out there in the bush. I said to Wendy, "How can you ever put out a thousand pots?" I'd put out twenty good ones and that'll be it. I'll replace them if somebody bought them, but I wouldn't have 1,000 pots out. She said yes, that he reeled them off. I said to him when he was standing out there, "Have you studied the Japanese potters from Kyoto?" "Oh, no," he said. "I wouldn't do that. I want to remain clear."

AV: Yes and I had to struggle to find two cups that could remotely be a pair and I finally found two that had spirals in the bottom that were roughly similar, but even those—the size was disproportionate and I understand exactly what you're saying. You spin off pot after pot or cup after cup and none of them are a pair and—

JC: None of them have finesse.

AV: That's right. There's a certain rustic quality to them, which I appreciate. But at the same time are they masterworks? No. Are they aspirational? No.

JC: That's the story of most young writers. They are trying to make a lot of pots because they think that that's how to have a career. One good book out of life is probably the best one can hope for—I think any really fine writer's only writing one book, constantly doing the same book over and over again, but in the process, he's deepening the well from which he draws, so it's a new book altogether but the ideas are essentially are the same. Whereas a public writer or an ordinary writer, he's writing a different book every time. New plot. New characters. Off we go. I say you've only got one book, but you're going to spend your lifetime getting it right.

AV: One truly great book—that's the aspiration.

JC: And even though you never know whether you're going to do it, because throughout the years—your 30s, your 40s, and your 50s even, you still think, "Oh. I haven't even got there." A frustrating experience after 25 or whatever years. And sometimes you settle for seconds. And you think the manuscript is ready, but thank God you don't publish it because you somehow think I'm going to freeze this text if I do. And if I do these right, why would I freeze it now? So that's what happened with the trilogy. I just wrote one. That was the end of it. I didn't think there were two other books that I might add. The two books came to me ultimately when I was in Amsterdam and I was sitting down once more working on the trilogy. It was a trilogy and I suddenly realized—could you? You've created these characters, but you haven't finished their lives. You haven't given us the ultimate expression of who they are, so almost within in a burst of time, I'd done the first of the sequels up there in Amsterdam and I realized that you definitely haven't finished the book because you've created three other characters—the young men that were the watchers—the ones that learned from—the watchers learning from the knowers, so I then knew that the third book was in it. But thankfully the second and the third books were not as hard to write because in a sense, I knew what I was doing absolutely and you've got to write. But that sense of getting it right for the master work and it's a master work for you. It's not a master work necessarily for a world view. It's you know that you've reached the limit of your powers and you cannot get better at it and that's the ultimate satisfaction I think as a writer to walk away from it and say, "I've got it. It's there. And I don't have to touch a word again." Somebody else can change it—comment here and there if they so wish, correct a spelling mistake, but ultimately people say to me, "You don't ever use an editor?" I say no. I don't need an editor. I will edit a book with fifty drafts. It doesn't go through one or two or five drafts. It's years of drafting before you get it and I find that very satisfying, I have to say. The drafting process is like a mechanic getting out there and letting the oil out of the thing and then he can start to work on the top end of the thing and pull it apart and get the gasket out. Put in new gaskets. To me, that's the deep technical side of literature: a writer is constantly working out the text and I'm sure people even in the past—I don't know what it's like to read Plato in the original Greek. I don't know if you do. Whether it's scruffy words or not, I don't know, but in translation of course by the great translators, he always sounds to me quite remarkable how they got it. Do you have any sense of that in terms of the greatness of things versus the translation of things?

AV: Are you driving at the idea of the clarity of the text?

JC: The polish of the text.

AV: The polish. It's an interesting question because Plato's works, except for the letters, are all dialogues. Was he polished in the sense of contemporary literature? I don't think so. And the same is true in a different way of Plotinus. Plotinus actually was not a writer. He, for the most part, left us notes written by someone else. The *Enneads* are notes and so it's filtered. What we're talking about is not exactly the same as what you're seeing with their work. A closer analogy might be Shakespeare, where Shakespeare was shaping his plays and the language of the plays to perfection and the precise word that's used is absolutely the precise word. And yet it all comes out of this creative efflorescence. This kind of lightning bolt of creativity, but then also crafted perfectly for the stage. I think what you're describing to some extent are different things—or referring to are different things in that—there is an element of linguistic precision to Plato or Plotinus. I'm not saying there isn't, but that's not the—it's not the same as creating the jewel of Yeats's poem "Sailing to Byzantium." The precise perfection that makes the confluence of those particular words the crown jewel of his work and I think that's part of what you were referring to. So in that sense, literature as you're talking about it is also like or analogous to painting for example. Capturing the light in a particular way that no one has captured before, as happened with the Hudson River School, or with painters of the sublime in Australia. It's perfection within that given canvas and space and I think that's something that distinguishes literature as we're thinking of it here, as distinct from philosophy. We're talking about the sublime in a different context.

JC: I agree with all of that. I agree with it. *On the Sublime* by Longinus, wasn't it?, who wrote a little book called *On the Sublime*, which had quite an effect upon me. I think that great literature is sublime.

AV: That's absolutely what I think. That's why I brought in the term "sublime," because for me, that ultimately it all comes together in order to create a sense of sublimity, a sense of exaltation-- we are exalted by participating in that work. There is something in it that brings us above life. That's true in *Moby*

Dick. That's true of Shakespeare. That's true of great poets and a great poem—there is something extraordinary there—and also a great painting. Truly great. There's something about it that exalts us. It exalts nature. We are exalted and we experience exaltation. And that I think is ultimately the test and it's the aspiration—the aspiration is also the test.

JC: And that's the element that's absolutely missing from contemporary art and contemporary literature. If you look at latest works that are coming through the art scene, they're mostly referential and they use the word "postmodern," which is a rather slippery term. But the work is referential and needs to be explained by the painter. We're going for something entirely different, and so to talk to the average artist who is doing this sort of work about the sublime would be probably giving them a sense of agitation because they definitely don't want to go there. They usually want to go to a political statement in a way. A lot of art today is politically stated. People say, "Well, all art has a political statement to make," and that's true. It does. Even the Impressionists, you could argue that they, with their requirement to touch and see things differently, were making a political statement about the ossification of our society that had already dug its heels in over neoclassicism, because they had no imagination for anything else, so they would toss a couple of gods on paper or employ a canvas that's 50 feet by 35 feet. Whereas many of those impressionists were painting small paintings, but they were looking for something sublime in their works. You only have to read the letters of Van Gogh to get the sense of a man absolutely obsessed with the sublime in everything—light, fire, and the energy of color—breaking color down, a bit like a scientist breaking down things into atoms and molecules. Here he is doing it with the beautiful picture of stars at night in Saint-Rémy-de-Provence—that lovely one where the cafe and the stars are all fluttering out. Nobody's caught stars ever on canvas like that. In fact, very few people have ever painted stars. It's not in the painter's palette, so to speak, but he did it. Because he saw the star as a sublime act of expression of the cosmos and he wanted to get it on the canvas and that's what you're talking about in terms of the nature of the sublime on paper. And to get that star on paper is a bit like, as you suggest, Shakespeare—in one or two lines, getting it down so perfectly that there's nobody that'll ever surpass it in terms of language and in terms of the sublime nature of the word that he's put on paper. His work is sublime. It's a different sort of context because most of his plays as we know—usually deal with death and mayhem and destruction, and the ordinary, but amongst all of that are the stars of Van Gogh that shine through the text and words. That's my understanding of what it is to be a good or great writer.

www.ingramcontent.com/pod-product-compliance
Lightning Source LLC
Chambersburg PA
CBHW021331090426
42742CB00008B/562

* 9 7 8 1 5 9 6 5 0 0 3 3 4 *